KIELER GEOGRAPHISCHE SCHRIFTEN

Begründet von Oskar Schmieder

Herausgegeben vom Geographischen Institut der Universität Kiel
durch C. Corves, R. Duttmann, W. Hoppe, R. Ludwig, G. v. Rohr
H. Sterr und R. Wehrhahn

Schriftleitung: P. Sinuraya

Band 113

REINHARD STEWIG

Proposal for Including the Bosphorus, a Singularly Integrated Natural, Cultural and Historical Sea- and Landscape, in the UNESCO World Heritage Inventory

KIEL 2006

IM SELBSTVERLAG DES GEOGRAPHISCHEN INSTITUTS
DER UNIVERSITÄT KIEL
ISSN 0723 – 9874
ISBN 3-923887-55-8

Bibliographische Information Der DeutschenBibliothek
Die Deutsche Bibliothek verzeichnet diese Publikation in der Deutschen Nationalbibliografie; detaillierte bibliografische Daten sind im Internet über http://dnb.ddb.de abrufbar.

ISBN 3-923887-55-8

The title-photo presents the Ortaköy mosque and part of the first Bosphorus bridge: land and sea, old and new, religion and technology, neo-baroque and plain modern – typical of the Bosphorus sea- and landscape.

Photo: Reinhard Stewig

Alle Rechte vorbehalten

Preface

The author of this publication paid his first visit to the city of Istanbul and the western part of Turkey in 1959 after a full week of driving in his own private car from his home city of Kiel and prolonged breaks at the several borders and for the procurement of a transit visa through Bulgaria in the city of Beograd, where he was questioned whether he belonged to the Germany of Adenauer or the Germany of Ulbricht.

In 1962 a field outing was organized for a group of geography students from the University of Kiel to the city of Istanbul and a geographical excursion tour of the western part of Turkey. Research started in the city of Istanbul on three subjects: the historical world city function of Istanbul and its predecessor Constantinople (STEWIG 1964), the development of the traditional oriental street pattern of the city of Istanbul to a cosmopolitan one (STEWIG 1964) and on the explanation of the cul-de-sac street pattern of oriental cities, exemplified by samples from Istanbul (STEWIG 1966); besides, the development of the old, historically important overland route to Istanbul across the Balkans was investigated (STEWIG 1965).

Thereafter scientific interest turned to the city of Bursa under several aspects of industrialization. After preliminary research on the industrial structure of that city (STEWIG 1970) the impact of industrialization on the city population was, in 1974, researched on the basis of extensive household interviews, 1356, with the help of Turkish and German students (STEWIG et al. 1980; STEWIG 1986). The results led, first, to general statements about the industrialization of Turkey (STEWIG 1972), later to a three volume description of the long-term formation of industrial society in Turkey (STEWIG 1998, 1999, 2000, 2004).

But the city of Istanbul was never forgotten. The excellent restoration work of historic monuments in that city accomplished by the Türkiye Turing ve Otomobil Kurumu under the outstanding leadership of its late director general Çelik Gülersoy led to a study of Istanbul's endogenous tourism (STEWIG 1986). And, more than thirty years after the investigation of the cul-de-sac street pattern of the city of Istanbul one of the samples was revisited and its redress described (STEWIG 1998).

Also, thirty years after the research of 1974, the city of Bursa was revisited to find out about the new structures which appeared since the growth of the city population from 330.000 in 1974 to 1.2 million in the year 2000. The long acquaintance with the city of Bursa and its historical importance for Turkey – the consecutive first six sultans of the Ottoman Empire having been entombed there in a way which structures by means of the necropolic complexes (Turkish sing.: külliye) until today the inner part of the city in a singular manner – urged me to suggest that the city, at least the inner part of it, should be included in the UNESCO World Heritage Inventory (STEWIG 2004).

At the same time my attention turned again to the fascinating city of Istanbul and its beautiful surroundings, especially the Bosphorus sea- and landscape. So, research was done on the long-time development of the urban traffic structure of Istanbul (STEWIG 2006) and on the historical and actual traffic functions of the Bosphorus (STEWIG 2006). The author's acquaintance with the city of Istanbul not falling behind that of the city of Bursa the next move was to propose a similar procedure of UNESCO ranking for Istanbul. The Topkapı Sarayı (museum), the St. Sophia/Aya Sofya (ex cathedral, museum), the Süleymaniye mosque complex and the great land wall of Theodorius II. already listed in the UNESCO World Heritage Inventory, the Bosphorus sea- and landscape, the combination of natural qualities, historical importance, cultural value and beautiful arrangement, is also well worth being included in the UNESCO World Heritage collection.

Contents

Preface		I
1	**General Introduction**	1
2	**Definition, Description and Delimitation of the Bosphorus Sea- and Landscape**	3
3	**The Natural Qualities of the Bosphorus Sea- und Landscape**	7
3.1	The geological and geomorphological origin of the Bosphorus sea- and landscape	7
3.2	The hydrographical conditions of the Bosphorus	8
3.3	The seismological hazards of the Istanbul region	11
3.4	The natural features of the upper Bosphorus	12
4	**The Bosphorus Sea- and Landscape as the Theatre of Legendary and Historical Events**	13
5	**The Cultural Qualities of the Bosphorus Sea- and Landscape**	17
5.1	The Topkapı Sarayı Section	18
5.2	The Golden Horn / Haliç Section	19
5.3	The Tophane Section	20
5.4	The Fındıklı-Kabataş Section	22
5.5	The Dolmabahçe Section	22
5.6	The Beşiktaş Section	24
5.7	The Çırağan Section	25
5.8	The Ortaköy Section	27
5.9	The Kuruçeşme-Arnavutköy-Bebek Section	28
5.10	The Rumeli Hisarı Section	30
5.11	The Emirgan-Istinye Section	31
5.12	The Yeniköy-Tarabya Section	33
5.13	The Büyükdere-Sariyer Section	35
5.14	The Rumeli Kavağı Section	35
5.15	The Haydarpaşa-Harem Section	36
5.16	The Üsküdar Section	38
5.17	The Kuzguncuk-Beylerbeyi-Çengelköy Section	41
5.18	The Kuleli-Vaniköy-Kandilli Section	43
5.19	The Anadolu Hisarı Section	45
5.20	The Kanlıca Section	47
5.21	The Bay of Beykoz Section (Çubuklu-Paşabahçe-Beykoz-Hünkar)	48
5.22	The Anadolu Kavağı Section	50

6	**The Process of Settlement and Suburbanization in the Bosphorus Sea- and Landscape**	51
6.1	The ancient Greek period	52
6.2	The ancient Roman period	52
6.3	The Middle Age Byzantine period	53
6.4	The early modern Ottoman period	55
6.5	The modern Republican period	58
7	**Evaluation**	63
7.1	The UNESCO World Heritage Convention and Operational Guidelines	63
7.2	Singularity and the Bosphorus sea- and landscape	65
7.3	Authenticity and the Bosphorus sea- and landscape	69
7.4	Integrity, integration and the Bosphorus sea- and landscape	69
7.5	Conclusion	71
8	**Publications**	72
9	**Photographic Documentation**	78

Photo 1: The southern entrance to the Bosphorus (left) and the Golden Horn, 2006 — 79

Photo 2: The first Bosphorus bridge (from 1973), 2006 — 79

Photo 3: The second Bosphorus bridge (from 1988) and the crooked bay of Istinye, 2006 — 79

Photo 4: The lower Bosphorus and the entrance to the Golden Horn (left), 1959 — 80

Photo 5: The lower Bosphorus and the entrance to the Golden Horn (left), 2006 — 80

Photo 6: The Dolmabahçe palace; in the background international hotels, 2006 — 81

Photo 7: The central section of the Dolmabahçe palace, 1959 — 81

Photo 8: The Dolmabahçe mosque, 1959 — 82

Photo 9: The Dolmabahçe clock tower, 1997 — 82

Photo 10: The Çırağan palace as a ruin, 1959 — 83

Photo 11: The Çırağan palace as a noble hotel, 2006 — 83

Photo 12: The Beylerbeyi palace, dwarfed by the first Bosphorus bridge, 2006 — 84

Photo 13: The Küçüksu palace, 2006 — 84

Photo 14: Section of Rumeli Hisarı, 1962 — 85

Photo 15: Rumeli Hisarı, 2006 — 85

Photo 16: Anadolu Hisarı behind several yalıs (from right to left): Komodor Remzi Paşa yalı, Ilyas Bey / Pink yalı, Şeyh Talat Efendi yalı (being renovatad), Manastırlı Ismail Hakkı Bey yalı, Köseleçiler yalı, 2006 — 86

Photo 17: Ruin of the Genoese castle (Yoros) above Anadolu Kavağı and the Marko Paşa villa in the Turkish naval base, 2006 — 87

Photo 18: Tophane (left), Nusretiye mosque (middle) and Kılıç Ali Paşa mosque (right), cut off from the Bosphorus by the new Salıpazarı quay, 2006. — 88

Photo 19: Kuleli Askeri Lisesi and Kuleli mosque below Büyük Çamlıca, 2006 — 89

Photo 20: Kışlası barracks above the container port at Harem – Haydarpaşa, 2006 — 89

Photo 21: The building of the Marmara University above the port of Istanbul at Harem – Haydarpaşa, 2006 — 89

Photo 22: The Haydarpaşa railway station, 2006 — 89

Photo 23: The Cihangir mosque in the Fındıklı Kabataş section, 2006 — 90

Photo 24: The Haydarpaşa mosque, 2006 — 90

Photo 25: The Şemsi Paşa mosque, at the water, and the Rum Mehmet Paşa mosque at Usküdar, 2006 — 91

Photo 26: The Iskender Paşa mosque and a radar surveillance tower at the Kanlıca landing stage, 2006 — 91

Photo 27: Arnavutköy, 1959 — 92

Photo 28: Arnavutköy, 2006 — 92

Photo 29: The oldest existing yalı, the Amcazade Hüseyin Paşa / Köprülü yalı in a dilapidated state, south of the second Bosphorus bridge, 2006 — 93

Photo 30: The Sait Halim Paşa yalı, Yeniköy, 2006 — 93

Photo 31: The Şehzade Burhanettin Efendi yalı, Yeniköy, 2006 — 94

Photo 32: The Ahmet Afif Paşa yalı, Yeniköy, 2006 — 95

Photo 33: The Feridun yalı, Yeniköy, 2006 — 96

Photo 34: Modern yalıs at Kandilli, below the Kandilli Kız Lisesi (ex Adile Sultan palace), 2006 — 97

Photo 35: The Asaf Paşa yalı (redbrown) and the Ahmet Rasim Paşa yalı (left) below the ex Khedive (viceroy) summer palace at Kanlica, 2006 — 98

Photo 36: The restored palace of Abas Hilmi Paşa, the former Khedive (viceroy) of Egypt, at Kanlica, 1985 — 98

Photo 37: Yalıs in a row, at the water, Yeniköy, 2006 — 99

Photo 38: Summer residence of the Austrian ambassy, south of Tarabya, 2006 — 100

Photo 39: Summer residence of the German ambassy, south of Tarabya, 2006 — 100

Photo 40: Summer residence of the Russian ambassy, Sariyer, 2006 — 100

Photo 41: Recreation at the landing stage of Kanlıca, 2006 — 101

Photo 42: Tourists at the landing stage of Sariyer, 2006 — 101

Photo 43: Recreation at the landing stage of Ortaköy, 2006 — 101

Photo 44: Waterside promenade between Üsküdar and Harem; Kız Kulesi and Topkapı Sarayı 2006 — 101

Photo 45: Dalyan (stationary installation) for catching fish, bay
of Beykoz, 1959 — 102

Photo 46: Pilot and fire fighting vessels at the bay of Istinye, 2006 — 102

Photo 47: Pasabahçe glass factory, 2006 — 102

Photo 48: Tankfarm at Çubuklu, 1985 — 102

Table of figures

Figure 1: The Bosphorus: General Outline — 2

Figure 2: The Distribution of the Average Speed of the North-South Surface Current of the Bosphorus — 9

Figure 3: Byzantine Settlement Locations on the Bosphorus and their Modern Turkish Names — 54

Figure 4: Istanbul and the Settlements on the Bosphorus in the Second Half of the 17th Century — 56

Figure 5: Population and the Settlements of the Bosphorus in the Second Half of the 17th Century — 57

1 General Introduction

The vast area of southeastern Europe and southwestern Asia, comprising large parts of two continents, is structured by a peculiar distribution of land and sea, which mutually penetrate each other: the Black Sea, the Bosphorus, the Sea of Marmara, the Dardanelles, the Aegean Sea and the eastern Mediterranean Sea are the maritime components, the Balkan and the Anatolian peninsulas, which protrude in Thrace and northwestern Anatolia in minor peninsulas, are the terrestrial components.

At the Bosphorus and the Dardanelles, the Straits, which mark the traditional, but out-dated boundaries of Europe and Asia within the area, southeastern Europe and southwestern Asia come into close contact. This situation embodies a great potential for maritime and terrestrial cross-traffic, running longitudinally through the Bosphorus and the Dardanelles from the Black Sea to the Mediterranean and crossing transversally the Bosphorus and the Dardanelles en route from Europe to the Orient and vice versa.

Historically there has always been a peg between southeastern Europe and southwestern Asia in the form of great cities, starting in the legendary past. From the third to the first millennium B.C. that city was ancient Troy on the Dardanelles. Later the location shifted to the Bosphorus for good. Constantinople on the Bosphorus grew – as the capital city of the East Roman, later the Byzantine Empire from 330 A.D. to 1453 – to become in the zenith of its political power the world city of an empire that encompassed large parts of both, southeastern Europe and southwestern Asia.

Istanbul on the Bosphorus, the successor city of Constantinople, was – as capital city of the Ottoman Empire from 1453 to the end of the First World War – in the zenith of its political power in the $16^{th}/17^{th}$ centuries – the world city of a similar empire that also comprised large parts of both, southeastern Europe and southwestern Asia.

Today Istanbul has developed to a mega city with a population of more than ten million inhabitants, dominating by its sheer size many regions of the area. Development on and around the Bosphorus is of very great historical depth and there have been several fundamental changes in the fields of society, culture and religion, social economy and technology, urban settlement and traffic.

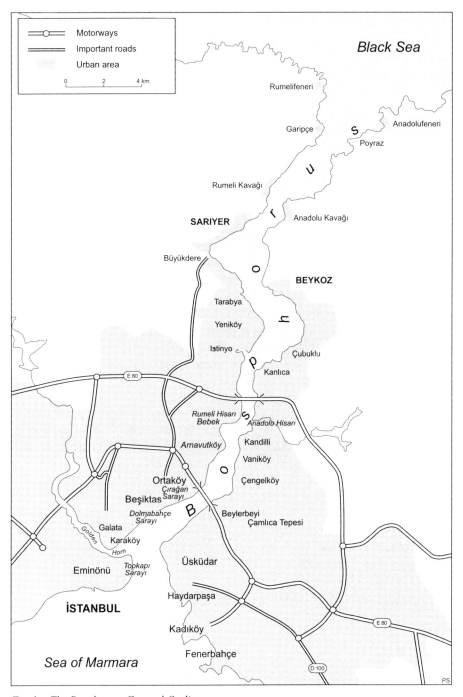

Fig. 1: The Bosphorus: General Outline
Source: Falkplan Istanbul, additional inset map

2 Definition, Description and Delimitation of the Bosphorus Sea- and Landscape

The Bosphorus (Turkish: Boğaziçi) is, first and foremost, a stretch of water, about 30 km long, connecting the Black Sea with the Sea of Marmara.

The Bosphorus is not a straight channel with parallel shore lines, it is rather of irregular shape. From the northern entrance to the middle section the Bosphorus changes its course in a rectangular way twice. In the middle section it winds a little and moves on in gentle curves to the southern entrance. This shape alone causes navigational hazards for shipping, the strong currents of the Bosphorus left out of account.

The irregularity of the Bosphorus's shape is further enhanced by the variability of narrow and wide passages. In the middle section, where the two suspension bridges stand, the Bosphorus is only about 600/700 meters wide. The northern entrance between Rumeli Feneri and Anadolu Feneri reaches a width of 3.5 km, the southern entrance is less wide, up to 1.8 km between Topkapı Sarayı and Harem.

In between there are a number of small and large bays which are used as anchorages for naval and merchant vessels as well as fishing and pleasure boats. The largest bays in the northern section are those of Büyükdere on the western and Beykoz-Paşabahçe on the eastern side, which widen the Bosphorus up to 3.5 km. Famous small bays on the western side are those of Istinye with a marina and Tarabya with a hotel.

Most of the small and large bays are to be found in places where little rivers flow down from the slopes and plateaus surrounding the Bosphorus and have cut narrow and wide valleys opening into the sea lane. Such little streams are in the north the Garipce Dere on the western and the Poyraz Dere on the eastern side. Farther south are the Büyükdere on the western and the famous Sweet Waters of Asia, Büyük and Küçük Göksu Dere, on the eastern side.

Of course, the Golden Horn (Turkish: Haliç) is a tributary of the Bosphorus, once the largest bay on the western side and was for a long time used as a harbour, but is today cut off from the Bosphorus by the old and new Galata Bridge, which – for our purposes – may be used as a delimitation of the Bosphorus in the southwest.

The northern and southern limits of the Bosphorus are fixed by lines between points where the coasts of the Black Sea and the Sea of Marmara turn in a rectangular way. The many small and large promontories and capes on both sides of the Bosphorus are arranged in such a way that a direct view from the southern to the northern entrance is obscured. Instead, the curves and turns of the Bosphorus together with the neighbouring high ground make up theatrical wings and contribute to the beautiful appearance.

The water area is, of course, the centre piece. But the Bosphorus sea- and landscape is not confined to the water area, the adjacent shores are an integral part of it. There are no natural sandy beaches. On the banks of the Bosphorus the slopes, some very steep, almost vertical, others moderately steep, still others with slight gradients, lead up to the plateaus extending on both sides. In many places no sharp edges between the slopes and the plateaus exist. The plateaus are generally level at an elevation of about 200 meters, in the north a little higher than in the south where they gently dip into the Sea of Marmara. There are some hills with moderate heights and soft contours on the plateaus, in the east more and a little higher than in the west.

The Büyük Çamlıca and the Küçük Çamlıca – both with telecommunication installations – rise up to 262 and 228 meters respectively, on the eastern side, opposite the old quarters of the city of Istanbul.

There is an extreme contrast between the slopes and plateaus of the northernmost Bosphorus and the rest. It is the contrast of nature and culture. On both sides of the northern section of the Bosphorus, in the west between Rumeli Feneri and Rumeli Kavağı, in the east between Anadolu Feneri and Anadolu Kavağı, the coasts are rugged and rocky, with steep slopes, precipitous cliffs, vertical in some places, often devoid of vegetation. The area is exposed to the relatively cold northeasterly winds (Turkish: poyraz – MANTRAN 1962, map 3) coming from the Black Sea. On the surrounding plateaus there is low vegetation. The strong and cold northerly winds prevent the Mediterranean climate to reach the coastline of the Black Sea and the northern Bosphorus with respective impacts on the vegetation. Settlements, mainly for technical purposes, like lighthouses, are few and isolated. There are no roads at the water's edge. The shores of the northern entrance to the Bosphorus are pure and attractive nature: not open to the public, a restricted military area (HINKLE & SLUIS 2003, p. 57). Schools of dolphins may be observed in the water, clouds of shearwaters, grey herons and black cormorants in the sky – a nature reserve (HINKLE & SLUIS 2003, p. 57). The wide bays of the northern Bosphorus are rich in fish, of which the swordfish (Turkish: kılıçbalığı) and the turbot (Turkish: kalkan) are the most prominent. Small and large fishing boats are numerous in the northern Bosphorus and there are also some stationary contraptions (Turkish sing.: dalyan) for catching fish.

What a contrast to the southern entrance to the Bosphorus. There, steep slopes exist too, even vertical ones between Kadıköy and Üsküdar, but generally the slopes have little inclination and the transition from the slopes to the plateaus is hardly perceptible.

There are strong winds there too, but they are warm and come from the southwest (Turkish: lodos – MANTRAN 1962, map 3) and this means that Mediterranean vegetation, though not on the plateaus, has the chance to establish itself in favourable spots. Cypress trees, chestnut trees, pine and plane trees dominate in the gardens.

But the main contrast is provoked by the complete coverage of the built-up areas at the water's edge, on the slopes and on the adjacent plateaus on both sides of the Bosphorus. These are areas where the development of settlements started with the foundation of ancient Calchedon (Turkish: Kadıköy) in 680 B.C. on the eastern and ancient Byzantion in 660 B.C. on the western side (MERLE 1916, p. 86). In the course of the long development since the first millennium B.C. the built-up areas were structured and re-structured time and again, but always remained built-up.

Today, the water's edge, the slopes and plateaus and the gently rolling hills are lined and covered with large and small palace-complexes, with large and small single palaces, with large and small pavilions (Turkish sing.: köşk), with mosque-complexes (Turkish sing.: külliye) and single mosques, with opulent and less opulent residences, with summer houses (Turkish sing.: yalı), with parks and gardens, with schools, training colleges and universities, with museums and hospitals, with restaurants and promenades, with prominent buildings and simple houses. Of course, there are also technical installations, landing jetties, marinas and ports, sometimes a little industry, and the water's edge is lined with roads, pedestrian precincts and recreation grounds. With the building areas ascending the slopes and hills along the contour lines it all appears as a beautiful arrangement of tiers facing the Bosphorus.

The middle section of the Bosphorus is a transition from the purely culturally structured southern to the purely naturally structured northern section, with some additional attractions like the restored ancient castles of Rumeli Hisarı and Anadolu Hisarı on the western and eastern sides respectively. Besides, on the western side is a stretch of stately buildings with gardens and parks: the summer residences of the foreign ambassadors to the Sublime Porte, which are today used by the consulates.

The built-up area is thinning out in northerly direction and refraining more and more from high ground. But the almost continuous line of settlements has already reached Büyükdere and Sariyer on the western side with more gardens and parks interspersed than in the southern section. On the eastern side the percentage of parks and gardens – and also of open spaces – is higher than on the western side, especially around the bay of Beykoz and industrial premises are to be found there.

The eastern side of the Bosphorus is a little longer exposed to the evening sun than the western side, with the disadvantage of early shadows. Where the indented shores of the small and large bays turn into an east-west direction there are favourable conditions for the siting of elegant and fashionable houses/summer residences on both sides of the Bosphorus.

The central axis of the Bosphorus sea- and landscape is of course the water area of the Bosphorus, but it has been clearly stated that the terrestrial surroundings are an integral part of the Bosphorus sea- and landscape. The question is: how far does this area reach inland? How and where is the Bosphorus sea- and landscape to be delimited away from the Bosphorus?

The famous Belgrade Ormanı is the only forest with high trees in the Istanbul region. It lies in the northwest, a little distance away from the Black Sea, about 5 km away from the Bosphorus on the plateau and is connected to the Bosphorus by the Büyükdere valley. The forest consists of 75% oak trees, 10% beech and chestnut trees, 5% hornbeam trees and other deciduous trees like alder, lime and elm; the percentage of coniferous trees is small. This is the vegetation typical of the temperate climate of central and western Europe.

Directly the Belgrade Ormanı has little to do with the Bosphorus, but it was and still is of great importance for the water supply of the city of Istanbul, in the past more than presently. It is also of great historical importance because it houses the famous seven water reservoirs (Turkish sing.: bend), which go back to Byzantine origin for the water supply of Constantinople and the reservoirs have been restored and cared for since early Ottoman times. Together with various aqueducts for carrying the water to Constantinople and Istanbul they are monuments of value and attractions – not only for tourists (MÜLLER-WIENER 1977, pp. 271-285, 514-518; STANDL 2003). The open question is: shall the Belgrade Ormanı be included in the Bosphorus sea- and landscape? Is it part of it?

The delimitation of the Bosphorus sea- and landscape is difficult to determine, especially when it comes to details. There are areas, mainly in the northern section of the Bosphorus, where a relatively clear edge exists between the slopes and the plateaus with obvious contrasts of the landscape. But in many places the parks and gardens and the built-up areas creep up the soft slopes and imperceptibly reach the plateaus where the sprawl of the urban settlement extends on both sides of the Bosphorus almost endlessly. The inland demarcation line of the Bosphorus sea- and landscape runs somewhere through the urban landscape of buildings and houses, a little nearer to the Bosphorus here, a little farther away there: as far as the slopes and hills and inclined plateaus face the Bosphorus – no matter what their land use may be – they belong to the Bosphorus sea- and landscape.

3 The Natural Qualities of the Bosphorus Sea- and Landscape

Of the physical features of the Bosphorus sea- and landscape the following will be considered: the geological and geomorphological, the hydrographical and the seismological aspects.

3.1 The geological and geomorphological origin of the Bosphorus sea- and landscape

The explanation of the Bosphorus as a geological and geomorphological formation, as a hollow form between raised plateaus, has its own peculiar history. The first attempt at a scientific interpretation saw the Bosphorus as a rift valley, i. e. of tectonic origin – an explanation which, at first sight, seems plausible because of the tectonic structures and frequent movements of the earth's crust in northwest Anatolia (BOIATZIS 1887; later: PENCK 1919).

But this view was soon altered. A. PHILIPPSON (1898) recognized the Bosphorus as a river valley – not unlike that of the river Rhine in Germany between the cities of Bingen and Koblenz – formed by fluviatile erosion. The question now was: what kind of river? Did it flow from the Black Sea to the Sea of Marmara or perhaps vice versa?

The discovery of a series of erosion terraces on both sides of the Bosphorus, some of them submerged, was a confirmation of the view that the Bosphorus had the character of a river valley. The erosion terraces showed an inclination in a northerly direction which meant that – if a river ever flowed in the Bosphorus valley – it must have run from south to north – i.e in the opposite direction of today.

It was also discovered that the level plateaus on both sides of the Bosphorus were – in the distant geological past–formed by denudation, which classifies the plateaus as peneplains (PENCK 1919).

The original geological situation – before the existence of the Bosphorus sea- and landscape – must have been that of a combined southeastern Thracian and northwestern Anatolian peneplain, into which a river and its tributaries started its dissecting erosion (PFANNENSTIEL 1944; KURTER & BENER 1962).

The final explanation of the origin of the Bosphorus (sea- and landscape) resulted in a more complicated situation: two rivers, a longer one flowing north, and a shorter one flowing south, did the erosion work and the world wide rise of the sea level at the end of the Ice Age filled the Bosporus valley with sea water (salt water). These two processes together are responsible for the formation of the Bosphorus sea- and landscape as it presents itself today, geologically, geomorphologically and hydrographically.

It was PENCK (1919) who introduced the two rivers in the explanation. The river that flowed north started from what are today the Alibeyköy and Kağıthane tributary rivers of the Golden Horn (Turkish: Haliç), flowed through the Golden Horn valley and turned north at a place that is today the entrance to the Golden Horn. The short river that flowed south started from a ridge which today runs – as a submarine ridge – across the southern entrance to the Bosphorus, from Sirkeci to Üsküdar, where the Kız Kulesi (Leander's Tower) pierces the sea level on a rock. This ridge was – in the geological past, before the world wide rise of the sea level at the end of the Ice Age – the water shed between the Black Sea (basin) and the Sea of Marmara (basin).

The rise of the sea level flooded the Black Sea (basin), the Sea of Marmara (basin), the Bosphorus and Golden Horn valleys and the ridge across the southern entrance to the Bosphorus. All this happened in the younger geological past in stages of transgression and regression of the sea. During some of these stages there seems to have been a watery connection between the Black Sea and the Sea of Marmara via the Golf of Izmit – Lake Sapanca – River Sakarya – "Bosphorus" (PFANNENSTIEL 1944; ERINÇ 1954; TUROĞLU 1996).

The submerged ridge across the southern entrance to the Bosphorus is today the location where the Bosphorus tunnel is being constructed. The site was first suggested for that purpose by PENCK in 1918 (STEWIG 2006).

3.2 The hydrographical conditions of the Bosphorus

The hydrographical features of the Bosphorus are also full of contrast. This applies to many aspects. The Bosphorus is not only a sea lane connecting the Black Sea with the Sea of Marmara but it is, at the same time, a river. This river – at least as far as the upper layer of its water body is concerned – flows from north to south. The reason is the distribution of precipitation and evaporation in the distant surroundings of the Bosphorus, in eastern Europe and in the southern Mediterranean. The big Russian rivers (Dnieper, Don) and the Danube, originating from areas of high precipitation and low temperatures, i. e. where precipitation prevails over evaporation, empty their (fresh)water into the Black Sea. In contrast to this situation the large area of the Mediterranean Sea and North Africa is characterised by extreme dryness and high temperatures. There, evaporation prevails over precipitation. The ensuing water deficit of the Mediterranean Sea is compensated by the influx of water through the Strait of Gibraltar and the Turkish Straits, one of which is the Bosphorus.

The average speed of the upper layers of the Bosphorus water rushing from north to south ranges from 1 to 4 knots, but varies considerably (Bundesamt für Seeschifffahrt and Hydrographie 2004, p. 224 – map). This depends partly on the cross-section of the Bosphorus. In the narrow passages the speed is high, 4 knots and more underneath the

The Natural Qualities of the Bosphorus Sea- and Landscape 9

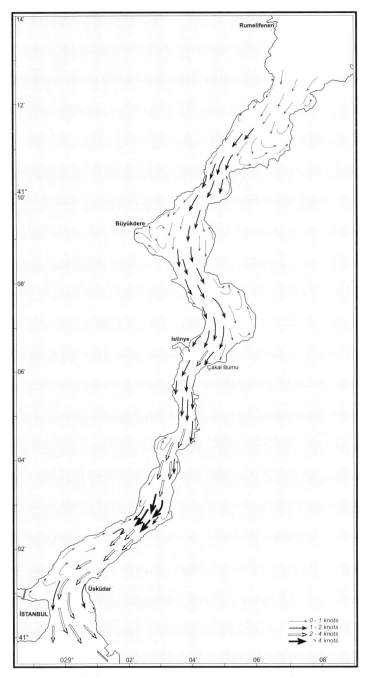

Fig. 2: The Distribution of the Average Speed of the North-South Surface Current of the Bosphorus
Source: Bundesamt für Seeschifffahrt und Hydrographie 2004, p. 224

first bridge, the Avrupa Köprüsü of 1973. In the northern and southern entrances to the Bosphorus as well as in the side bays the current is much slower.

On the other hand strong northeasterly winds (Turkish: poyraz) and strong southwesterly winds (Turkish: lodos) are of influence. The poyraz accelerates the surface water speed up to 7 knots, so that boats with insufficient engine power have difficulties in moving northwards. Rowing boats are said to have been transported over land to avroid the strong currents around some of the capes. A strong lodos has the effect of reducing the speed of the surface current.

There are other spectacular features of the surface current of the Bosphorus: maelstroms, stationary rotating water bodies, deep pools. Near the cape of Kandilli a depth of 110 meters is reached (HINKLE & SLUIS 2003, pp. 5, 77). Following the transition from narrow to wide passages some of the water whirls round, rotates and partly flows in the opposite direction. Where the concave coastline is to the right of the mainstream, the rotation turns clockwise to the right, where it is to the left it turns counter-clockwise left (Bundesamt für Seeschifffahrt und Hydrographie 2004, p. 224 – map). These situations cause difficulties for the navigation of ships, especially the Bosphorus ferries during their approach to the landing jetties. With all this the spectacular hydrographical features of the Bosphorus do not end.

An extreme contrast within the water body of the Bosphorus is the existence of two currents, an upper or surface current and a lower or bottom current (MERZ & MÖLLER 1928). These currents run in 180 degrees opposite flow directions, one on top of the other (see also HINKLE & SLUIS 2003, p. 5). Though the existence of a bottom current had already been observed in 1681, it was denied even in 1871 (MERZ & MÖLLER 1928, p. 11). But the fact was later generally accepted by ocea-nographers, one of them a Russian naval officer, S. MAKAROFF, in 1885, who started the first thorough investigation, which was, in 1917/1918, elaborated and perfected by MERZ & MÖLLER (1928).

The contrast between the Black Sea and the Mediterranean Sea is not only that of diffe-rent relations between precipitation and evaporation, but also that of different saline content of the water. The high evaporation in the Mediterranean Sea area increases the saline content of the sea water, while the big Russian rivers (Dnieper, Don) and the Danube empty freshwater into the Black Sea. The surface current of the Bosphorus carries the warm freshwater from the Black Sea, the bottom current the heavier and cold saline water from the Mediterranean Sea (HINKLE & SLUIS 2003, p. 5).

The saline content of the surface current of the Bosphorus amounts only from 16 and 18‰ to 20‰ from north to south (MERZ & MÖLLER 1928, p. 224). The saline content of the bottom current, which creeps over the submarine ridge in the southern entrance to the Bosphorus, decreases from about 38‰ in a depth of 30 meters above the ridge to 30 and 35‰ in a depth of 70 meters in the northern entrance to the Bosphorus – along the moderate south - north gradient of the (submarine) valley floor of the Bosphorus (MERZ & MÖLLER 1928, p. 225).

The speed of the bottom current is generally less than that of the surface current, between 30, 50 and 100 cm/sec., according to MERZ & MÖLLER (1928), depending on the wide and narrow passages.

There is an important hydrographical pre-condition for the existence of palaces, summer residences (Turkish sing.: yalı), buildings and houses right at the water's edge: the lack of tidal action in the Bosphorus, the pronounced stability of the water level with little fear of flooding (HINKLE & SLUIS 2003, pp. 5, 41).

Besides, the different qualities of the water, temperature and saline content, encourage regular migrations of fish between the Mediterranean and the Black Sea and vice versa, mainly in April/May and September/October. This is the natural basis of the extensive fishing industry on the Bosphorus (HINKLE & SLUIS 2003, p. 6) and the many fish restaurants at the shores.

3.3 The seismological hazards of the Istanbul region

Other spectacular natural features – not only of the Bosphorus, but the whole of the Istanbul region (and beyond) – are the extreme seismological hazards (ERCAN 2001). This is due to the existence of plate tectonics. Only a few kilometers south of the southern entrance to the Bosphorus, south of the Princes's Islands (Turkish: Kızıl Adalar), the floor of the Sea of Marmara drops down in a steep escarpment to a depth of 1200 meters (MERZ & MÖLLER 1928, p. 10; ARDEL & KURTER 1970-1971). This is part of the North Anatolian Fault Line (PAVONI 1961; KETIN 1969) which runs as a rather straight line, a zone, 50 to 100 km wide, from the eastern border of Turkey to the western and through the northern Sea of Marmara. It is connected with heavy earthquakes. These are caused by the fact that two different tectonic plates clash along the North Anatolian Fault Line: a northern one and a southern one, which move – slowly but surely – in opposite directions. The friction generated by this movement is released in heavy earthquakes, the last of which happened in 1999 twice in Izmit and in Düzce, magnitude 7.4 and 7.2. The earth strikes killed 1000 people in Avcılar, a western suburb of Istanbul built on soft rock, 100 km away from the epicenters.

The Istanbul region and the Bosphorus area have been hit by heavy earthquakes, sometimes combined with seismic waves (tsunamis), since time immemorial (ERCAN 2001, pp. 52-54). The last very heavy earthquake in Istanbul occurred in 1894 (EGINITIS 1895).

Earthquake forecasting is a difficult business, but knowledge about earthquakes in the past, their locations, magnitudes and recurrence periods allows for probability forecasts. According to PARSONS et al. (2000, p. 664) there is "a 62 ± 15% probability of strong shaking in greater Istanbul over the next 30 years (May 2000 to May 2030)", a "50 ± 13% over the next 22 years, and a 32 ± 12% over the next 10 years".

The impending earthquake hazard of the city of Istanbul and the Bosphorus with its tunnel under construction is a lasting infamous natural quality of the Bosphorus sea- and landscape (STEWIG 2006).

3.4 The natural features of the upper Bosphorus

The intension of this publication is to explain why the Bosphorus sea- and landscape should be included in the UNESCO World Heritage Inventory. A distinction is made by the UNESCO in the World Heritage Convention between natural and cultural phenomena of world ranking. Surely, the Bosphorus sea- and landscape as a whole is an integrated combination of natural and cultural features. In the lower and middle sections the sea- and landscape is covered by a multitude of extraordinary human settlements.

But, when the shores of the Bosphorus sea- and landscape are to be divided into natural and cultural areas the sea fronts of the uppermost northern section of the Bosphorus, from Rumeli Kavağı to Rumeli Feneri on the western side and from Anadolu Kavağı to Anadolu Feneri on the eastern side, are – this has been stated in the previous descriptive chapter–exclusively dominated by natural phenomena. This is an obvious contrast to all other areas. However, the combination of such neighbouring contrasts together make up the complete and integrated whole of the Bosphorus sea- and landscape.

4 The Bosphorus Sea- and Landscape as the Theatre of Legendary and Historical Events

The following text is not meant to be a history of the Bosphorus, it is not intended as a consecutive series of historical facts, nor is it following a time-related chronology, but it is a guideline – as befits the spatial aspect of the investigation – along the various locations of the Bosphorus and their connection with historical and/or legendary events.

The legend about the name of the Bosphorus

Already the name of the Bosphorus is of legendary origin. The superior ancient Greek god Zeus had a love-affair with Io, the daughter of an ancient king. This aroused the jealousy of Hera, Zeus' wife. To conceal her Io was transformed into a young cow. But Hera pursued her with a gadfly. To escape Io plunged into the sea lane between the Black Sea and the Sea of Marmara, which took on the name of the Bosphorus, i. e. Ford of the Cow (SUMNER-BOYD & FREELY 1972, p. 473).

The legendary voyage of the Argonauts

The northern entrance to the Bosphorus is connected with the legendary voyage of the Argonauts from the Aegean Sea into the Black Sea through the Bosphorus to recover the Golden Fleece. The legend recounts that it was difficult to leave the Bosphorus because of the Semplegades, the clashing rocks (Turkish: Öreke Taşı), closing the sea lane from time to time. It is the location where precipitous cliffs exist on both sides of the northern entrance to the Bosphorus. Having let a dove make a test flight, which just managed to succeed, Jason, the leader, and his ship Argo, together with a number of ancient Greek heroes, got through (SUMNER-BOYD & FREELY 1972, pp. 473, 496).

The legends about the Kız Kulesi (Leander's Tower)

At the southern entrance to the Bosphorus two legends are connected with the Kız Kulesi (literally translated: Maiden's Tower, also named Leander's Tower). A general legend has it that a father, having knowledge of the prophecy that his daughter will be killed by a snake-bite, had her sent to the tower, isolated by the water of the Bosphorus. Yet she met her death from a serpent which reached the small island in a basket of fruit (SUMNER-BOYD & FREELY 1972, p. 431).

There exists another version of this legend (MEYER 1908, p. 313): the girl is a princess and the daughter of Sultan Mehmet and there is a happy ending: her lover succeeds in sucking the poison from the wound and saves her.

The other legend wrongly connected with this Kız Kulesi refers to the swimming adventure of Leander, who drowned trying to reach his beloved hero. If this ever happened the place was not the Bosphorus but the Dardanelles (SUMNER-BOYD & FREELY 1972, p. 431).

The crossing of Darius in 515 B.C.

A non-fictitious, historical event of pre-Christian times is connected with another location of the Bosphorus: the building of a bridge of boats – an enormous innovation at the time – in 513 B. C. by Darius I., a Persian king on his military endeavours into the Balkans and across the Bosphorus. SUMNER-BOYD & FREELY (1972, p. 488) believe this to have happened in the narrows of the Bosphorus at the present site of Rumeli Hisarı. Darius is supposed to have watched the crossing of his several thousand men from a throne which still existed in antiquity.

The slip-way for boats across Beyoğlu in 1453

In 1453 the Byzantine Empire had been reduced to the city of Constantinople which covered at the time the triangular area between the Golden Horn, the Sea of Marmara and the Bosphorus and a small settlement across the Golden Horn, Galata. These areas were protected by land and sea walls; the defenders had closed the entrance to the Golden Horn by a floating chain unsurpassable for boats or ships. Sultan Mehmet II. (1451-1481) who conquered the city and was given the title Fatih (English: conqueror) for his achievement, had the most advanced artillery of the time, able to cut breaches into the strong land walls, but was – because of the long the sea fronts of the city – unable to advance on several fronts simultaneously. The Golden Horn closed by a chain he created a spectacular detour to overcome the obstacle: a number of ships were moved up the hill of around 70 meters just outside Galata on a wooden slipway, pulled by oxen, and then lowered down the hill on the other side to Kasimpaşa on the Golden Horn (NICOLLE & HOOK 2000, pp. 57-62; SUMNER-BOYD & FREELY 1972, p. 471).

The starting place was on the western side of the Bosphorus, probably at the mouth of a little valley where the Dolmabahçe mosque and the Dolmabahçe Saat Kulesi (English: clock tower) now stand at the water's edge below the Hilton Hotel and the İnönü Stadyumu. The defenders of Constantinople, attacked on an additional front, were unable to protect both sea and land walls and had to succumb. The event is today commemorated by a folkloristic show of boats being pulled across Beyoğlu on almost the old route.

The legend about the name of Çubuklu from Evliya Çelebi (1611-1685)

Çubuklu is the name of a settlement on the eastern side of the Bosphorus between Kanlıca and Paşabahçe. Its name may be explained by a legend. There, Sultan Beyazıt II. (1489-1512) – in a fit of anger – gave eight strokes to his son, who later became Sultan Selim

I. Yavuz (1512-1520) with a cane (Turkish: çubuk), meaning his fruitful future reign of eight years. To ascertain the quality of the cane he struck it into the ground. The cane took root and began to bear fruit. The legend was related by Evliya Çelebi (1611-1685), the famous Turkish traveller (SUMNER-BOYD & FREELY 1972, p. 502).

The Treaty of Hünkar Iskelesi of 1833

Not far from Çubuklu, also on the eastern side of the Bosphorus, a little to the northwest of Beykoz, is Hünkar Iskelesi (English: the Sultan's landing jetty), deeply related to historical facts. After the Ottoman Empire had passed its zenith of political power in the $16^{th}/17^{th}$ centuries and since the retreat of the Ottoman Empire from the northern shores of the Black Sea Russia began to expand southwards, trying to gain entrance to the Mediterranean Sea via the Bosphorus. The drive continued even after the dissolution of the Soviet Union in the nineteen nineties. The Turco-Egyptian War of 1831-1833, ending with a weak position of the Ottoman Empire, induced the Sublime Porte to look for help. This resulted in the Treaty of Hünkar Iskelesi in 1833 which allowed Russian soldiers to be stationed for some time nearby (von MOLTKE 1893, map of the Bosphorus: the Russian camp) and opened the Bosphorus to Russian ships (SUMNER-BOYD & FREELY 1972, p. 500; SHAW & SHAW 1977, pp. 32-35).

The work of Florence Nightingale in 1854

There were many struggles between the Ottoman Empire and Russia, one of them was the Crimean War from 1853 to 1856, between Russia on the one side and the Ottoman state together with its allies Britain and France on the other side. The Bosphorus was the base line for the fighting that took place on the northern shore of the Black Sea.

A military hospital at Haydarpaşa, at the eastern side of the southern entrance to the Bosphorus, became the sphere of activity of Florence Nightingale (1820-1910) who arrived there in 1854 together with a number of nurses. They managed to reduce the mortality-rate and to improve hygiene; they cared not only for British soldiers but for the French as well (SWEETMAN 2001, pp. 60-65). Her work may be considered as the immediate forerunner of that of H. Dunant, who in 1863 founded the International Red Cross.

The three sultans of the year 1876

The exodus of the ruling Ottoman family in the middle of the 19th century from their long-time residence and political centre, the Topkapı Sarayı, on the western side of the southern entrance to the Bosphorus, on a spur of high ground, the site of ancient Byzantion, and their move to the newly opened palaces of Dolmabahçe (1853-1856), Çırağan (1863-1871) and Beylerbeyi (1865) on the western and eastern sides of the Bosphorus effected that several modern political events are connected with the Bosphorus sea- and landscape (KREISER 2001, pp. 225-230). An important year was 1876. In this year three sultans ruled the Ottoman state.

Sultan Abdülaziz (1861-1876) – accused of despotism – was dethroned by a military coup (KREISER 2001, p. 226). For him Sultan Murat V. (1876) took over. But it turned out that he was mentally ill, so that it was finally his younger brother Abdülhamit II. (1876-1909) who was enthroned as sultan. Abdülaziz committed suicide in 1876 in the Çırağan palace (KREISER 2001, p. 228).

The Çırağan incident of 1878

But the conspiracies around the Bosphorus palaces did not end with the suicide. The mother of the deposed Murat V. spun her intrigues trying to get her son back on the throne. Her endeavours resulted in what has been termed the Çırağan incident of 1878. But the leader of the conspirators was killed in the Çırağan palace by an officer of the watch (KREISER 2001, pp. 228-230). Murat was allowed to reside in the Çırağan palace where he died in 1904.

When Abdülhamit II. (1876-1909) was dethroned by the Young Turks Revolution of 1908, the Çırağan palace served as the meeting place of the new Turkish Parliament in 1909, but not for long: it burned down in 1910 (KREISER 2001, p. 230) and remained in ruins for a very long time, until it was partly restored since 1991 as an extra-class noble hotel of the Kempinski-Group (GORYS 2003, p. 189).

The death of Atatürk at Dolmabahçe in 1938

The Dolmabahçe palace was used by Mustafa Kemal Paşa, Atatürk, when he was in Istanbul and not in Turkey's new capital city Ankara. Atatürk died in the Dolmabahçe palace in 1938 (SUMNER-BOYD & FREELY 1972, p. 471).

The state visitors at the Bosphorus palaces

The beautiful Bosphorus sea- and landscape served as the proper setting for state visits to the Ottoman Empire and Turkey. The Empress Eugénie of France, the Emperor Franz Josef of Austria, the Shah Nasireddin of Persia and Edward VIII. of Britain together with Mrs. Simpson stayed at the Beylerbeyi palace (SUMNER-BOYD & FREELY 1972, p. 508). The German Kaiser Wilhelm II., Winston Churchill and Charles de Gaulle resided at the Şale Köşkü in the Yıldız Parkı, behind the Çırağan palace (GORYS 2003, p. 164).

The many legendary and real historical events of international rank connected with the Bosphorus and its surroundings, of which the above mentioned are a cross-section, are illustrative aspects of the invisible dimension of the cultural qualities of the Bosphorus sea- and landscape.

5 The Cultural Qualities of the Bosphorus Sea- and Landscape

The material manifestations of the cultural qualities of the Bosphorus sea- and landscape are expressed in a multitude of installations. There are large and small, opulent and plain palaces; there are summer residences (Turkish sing.: yalı, pl. yalılar), ranging from small palaces, detached and surrounded by gardens and parks, with sites right at the water's edge to simple houses in a row, with a coastal road between the houses and the water; there are religious institutions, representative mosques with additional buildings (Turkish sing.: külliye) and unintentional neighbourhood mosques; there are educational institutions, a variety of museums, high ranking schools, training colleges and universities; there are recreational institutions, promenades, pedestrian precincts, restaurants, coffee-houses and tea-gardens; there are traffic installations for the port traffic of Istanbul, for the ferry traffic across the Bosphorus and for the transit shipping on the sea lane.

Of all these the summer residences, which form a majority, attracted elaborate scientific attention. The city authorities of Istanbul (ERDENEN 1993/1994) published a four volume manual about the (Turkish) sahilhaneler (English: shore houses; cp. HINKLE & SLUIS 2003, p. 41). The architectural aspects were delineated in a two volume publication by ELDEM 1993, 1994). The artistic viewpoint was revealed in the – with colour photos – well furnished publication by HELLIER & VENTURI (1993 and 1994). And there is a helpful little book by HINKLE & SLUIS (2003) – helpful for the identification and location of more summer residences than can be considered in the following text – with a systematic collection of (small) colour photos of the summer residences; 76 yalıs are listed in the index. In the compendium of shore houses (Turkish: sahilhaneler) by ERDENEN (1993/1994) 365 are registered and delineated (with architectural plans and old and new photos, 835 pages), 173 on the Thracian, 192 on the Anatolian side.

Of the total length of 30 km of the Bosphorus the northernmost 6 km on both, the western, Thracian side, from Rumeli Kavağı to Rumeli Feneri, and on the eastern, Anatolian side, from Anadolu Kavağı to Anadolu Feneri – as has already been stated – are an almost purely natural sea- and landscape.

On the large rest, 24 km on the Thracian and 24 km on the Anatolian side, i. e. 48 km in all, the cultural phenomena of the Bosphorus sea- and landscape extend in manifold variety and – in several places – in symmetrical arrangement on both sides of the Bosphorus. The great number of phenomena, the wide range of different qualities and the length of the shore line demand subdivision: 22 sections may be distinguished, 14 on the western, 8 on the eastern side.

5.1 The Topkapı Section

First, it has to be remembered that the Topkapı Sarayı, which was for nearly 400 years, from the end of the 15th to the middle of the 19th century, the residence of the ruling Ottoman family, is already listed in the UNESCO World Heritage Inventory. The Topkapı Sarayı with its many residential, recreational and service buildings, its gardens and walls (MÜLLER-WIENER 1977, pp. 495-507), originally extended over 70 hectares (0,7 km^2). It was changed into a museum in 1924 after the Ottoman rulers had left the palaces in the middle of the 19th century.

The area of the Topkapı Sarayı covered and still covers the spur of land that protrudes from the Thracian peninsula and is surrounded on three sides by the Sea of Marmara, the Golden Horn and the Bosphorus. The eastern–northeastern to southeastern–slopes of the Topkapı Sarayı face the Bosphorus and consequently this area is part of the Bosphorus sea- and landscape. It is the spur of land where Greek colonists from Megara planted the acropolis of the city of Byzantion in 660 B.C. (MERLE 1916, p. 86) and it reminds the spectator of 2600 years of history, though nothing of the first settlement remains. Together with the little earlier foundation of the colony of Calchedon in 680 B. C. (MERLE 1916, p. 86) – opposite the acropolis of Byzantion – the entire development of settlements of the Bosphorus sea- and landscape started – symmetrically – at its southern entrance.

The lower slopes of the Topkapı Sarayı are lined by a sea wall which extends beyond the area along the Sea of Marmara and originally also along the Golden Horn (MÜLLER-WIENER 1977, pp. 312-319). The sea walls go back to Byzantine times, but they were repaired and renewed by the Ottomans because the city of Istanbul was several times in danger of being attacked by the fleets of the Italian merchant cities of Venice and Genoa (MÜLLER-WIENER 1977, pp. 314-316). The sea walls had several gates and towers. In 1755 a lighthouse (Turkish: fener), which still exists, was added at the edge of the entrance to the Bosphorus (MÜLLER-WIENER 1977, p. 502). The sea wall also protected what was once a garden of the Topkapı Sarayı and is since 1913 a public park (Turkish: Gülhane Parkı) (MÜLLER-WIENER 1977, p. 504).

Parts of the sea wall along the Bosphorus still exist, though in some sections railway and road construction destroyed the alignment. The (single) railway line of 1871 followed the least gradient on a terrace behind the sea wall. More destruction was caused by the construction of a second rail track in 1940 (MÜLLER-WIENER 1977, p. 318). For the adjustment of the city of Istanbul to the growing motor traffic in the 1960ties a peripheral road (Turkish: Sahil Yol/Kennedy Caddesi) was laid out in front of the sea wall in 1959 (MÜLLER-WIENER 1977, p. 318).

But the pittoresque situation is little impeached: the sea wall conceals the rail track and the road is almost level with the sea. Above the sea wall rise the outer walls of the Topkapı

Sarayı. From different angles of the Bosphorus the famous skyline of the oldest quarters of the city of Istanbul may be observed and the panoramic view adds to the pittoresque character of the area: the Aya Sofya Museum (ex St. Sophia cathedral – MÜLLER-WIENER 1977, pp. 84-96) with its four, a little clumsy minarets, the Sultan Ahmet mosque with its six admirably slim minarets (MÜLLER-WIENER 1977, pp. 470-474), some towers and domes and stacks of the kitchen tract of the Topkapı Sarayı (MÜLLER-WIENER 1977, pp. 495-507).

The cape (Turkish: Saray Burnu) where the Golden Horn meets the Bosphorus is today a public park, crowned by a statue of Atatürk (Turkish: Atatürk Heykeli). The Topkapı Sarayı section of the Bosphorus sea- and landscape is a combination of quiet historical and scenic attractions.

5.2 The Golden Horn (Turkish: Haliç) Section

This section comprises the entrance area from the Bosphorus to the Golden Horn and is delimited by the Galata Bridge. As long as no bridges existed across the Haliç the Golden Horn was the largest bay of the Bosphorus into which the two little tributary rivers, the Alibeyköy and the Kağıthane, emptied what was called the Sweet Waters of Europe. Before bridges were built the cross traffic between the oldest quarters of the city south of the Golden Horn and the fast growing modern areas in the north (Galata, Pera—Beyoğlu) was managed by boats and many piers existed on both sides of the Haliç (MÜLLER-WIENER 1977, pp. 126-127; STEWIG 2006).

The present Galata bridge, a draw bridge, is a bascule bridge dating from 1992. It had several forerunners, the first was constructed in the middle of the 19th century (MÜLLER-WIENER 1977, p. 138). The bridge opened in 1912 was a pontoon bridge with many pillars, hampering the outflow of the Golden Horn and contributing to the pollution of its water. The pontoons of the middle section of the bridge were tugged away in the early hours every morning to allow ships to pass – the Golden Horn was, until recently, the main harbour of Istanbul and the foremost location of industy (MÜLLER-WIENER 1988; STANDL 1994). The new bridge – being a draw bridge – avoids the use of tugs; its slim pillars, which are supposed to withstand earthquakes, improve the circulation of the Haliç water.

The Galata bridge connects two focal points of inner urban traffic on the western side of the Bosphorus: Eminönü in the south and Karaköy in the north. The traffic importance of Eminônü is further enhanced by the existence of the main railway station on the western side of the Bosphorus, Sirkeci, nearby.

Admittedly the entrance area to the Golden Horn is a very functional part of the Bosphorus sea- and landscape: it is the passenger port of Istanbul and as such not – by all means – of value for the UNESCO World Heritage Inventory. However some points of historical interest exist: the Galata Bridge itself is a piece of modern technical history (MÜLLER-WIENER 1977, pp. 138-141) and there is the underground mosque (Turkish: Yeraltı camii) in Karaköy, originally a Byzantine dungeon where the chain across the Golden Horn was fastened. The Galata Tower (Turkish: Galata Kulesi) (MÜLLER-WIENER 1977, pp. 320-323) up the hill of Galata serves as a landmark for ships on the Bosphorus. Within the area of the passenger port (LEITNER 1965, 1967) the Eminönü and the Karaköy piers operate the commuter shipping traffic across the Bosphorus, to the Princes's Islands (Turkish: Kızıl Adalar), to the various suburbs on both sides of the Bosphorus and to several destinations on the coast of the Sea of Marmara. North of Karaköy the Salıpazarı quay is reserved for passenger ships, liners and cruise liners. Because of the limited quay space mooring buoys were anchored in the water (LEITNER 1967, table after p. 97 and map after p. 96), which are now gone.

However functional the character of the Golden Horn section of the Bosphorus sea- and landscape may be, the uninterrupted heavy shipping traffic of the traditional ferries (TEDSTONE 1986; AUSTIN 1995) and modern water busses and the colourful liner traffic contribute to the pittoresque atmosphere of the area.

5.3 The Tophane Section

The area of the Tophane section centres on a group of heterogeneous buildings standing relatively close to each other (SUMNER-BOYD & FREELY 1972, p. 460 – map; HÖGG 1967, pp. 319-327) and contrasting fundamentally, historically and architecturally.

Tophane was the name giving institution, a canon foundry, a gun manufactury. It was Sultan Mehmet II. Fatih (1451-1481), the conqueror of Constantinople, who founded Tophane just outside the walls of Galata, the ancient suburb on the northern side of the Golden Horn (MÜLLER-WIENER 1977, p. 321 – map). Being a military institution the place was originally surrounded by barracks (MÜLLER-WIENER 1977, p. 356) which characterised this faubourg right into the 18th/19th centuries. The Tophane of Mehmet II. was rebuilt, expanded and restored several times, by Beyazıt II. (1481-1512) and Selim III. (1789-1807) (SUMNER-BOYD & FREELY 1972, pp. 466-467) and the present relatively small building with its domes and stacks is waiting to be re-opened as a military museum (MÜLLER-WIENER 1977, p. 356).

Of greater cultural importance are the mosques, the Kılıç Ali Paşa mosque and the Nusretiye mosque (SUMNER-BOYD & FREELY 1972, pp. 464-468). The first is the foundation of a high ranking Ottoman naval officer and was built from 1578-1583 (MÜLLER-WIENER 1977, p. 430, groundplan on p. 431). It is a classical complex, a (Turkish) külliye, consisting of the mosque (Turkish: cami), the theological school (Turkish: medrese), a bath house (Turkish: hamam) and the mausoleum (Turkish: türbe) of the founder. There had also been a little fountain (Turkish: sebil) (MÜLLER-WIENER 1977, p. 430).

One of the outstanding architectural features is that the complex was built by the most famous Ottoman architect, Sinan (1490/91-1588) – in his old age. It has been criticized that it is a small replica of Aya Sofya/St. Sophia with its combination of longitudinal and central hall (SUMNER-BOYD & FREELY 1972, p. 464).

There is a small mosque, the Karabaş mescidi, of early date (1530) nearby, which was restored in 1992 (SUMNER-BOYD & FREELY 1972, p. 464). The other contrasting mosque is the Nusretiye camii (SUMNER-BOYD & FREELY 1972, p. 467). Nusretiye means victory and it was founded by Mahmut II. (1730-1754), the reformer sultan, to celebrate his victory over the Janissaries (by liquidation), an elite military corps which had developed into a state within the state. The architect, Kirkor Balyan (1764-1831), belonged to the family of famous Armenian architects who favoured what has been termed the Ottoman renaissance architectural style (SUMNER-BOYD & FREELY 1972, p. 467).

There is a baroque fountain, the Tophane çeşmesi, nearby, built by Mahmut I. (1730-1754) (SUMNER-BOYD & FREELY 1972, p. 466; cp. MÜLLER-WIENER 1977, p. 431).

Not far from the Nusretiye mosque stands a stubby little clock tower dating from the time of Abdülmecit I. (1839-1861) (KREISER 2001, p. 181). It is presently (2006) in a dilapidated condition.

Tophane and the Karabaş mescidi, the two mosques and the fountain are seperated today by modern road construction since 1959 (Nusretiye Caddesi) (MÜLLER-WIENER 1977, p. 356) and the introduction of light rail transport – (Turkish) tramvay – nowadays.

The worst disgrace, however, is caused by the extension of the Salıpazarı quay with its large store houses and customs office buildings in a northerly direction on reclaimed ground. Consequently the famous Kılıç Ali Paşa külliye with the türbe of a high ranking Ottoman naval officer fittingly originally at the water's edge is now concealed from the Bosphorus – only the tops of the minarets of the two mosques can be seen from a ship on the Bosphorus. The best view of the whole arrangement is from the Galata Tower.

Port traffic increasing and quay space in great demand it cannot be hoped that the old splendours of the Bosphorus sea- and landscape in this section – the mosques and their surroundings at the water's side – will be restored in such a way that they face the Bosphorus directly.

5.4 The Fındıklı-Kabataş Section

In contrast to the Tophane section and the outstanding Dolmabahçe section a little farther to the north the Fındıklı-Kabataş section is not a conspicuous area. It takes its reputation within the Istanbul region mainly from technical installations.

From the time of the growing number of motor vehicles in Istanbul in the 1960ties to the opening of the first suspension bridge across the Bosphorus in 1973 Kabataş was the main ferry port for cars to Üsküdar on the eastern side of the sea lane. Although there was day and night service and 17 ferries employed the ships could not cope with the enormous traffic which crowded – with long queues of cars – the costal roads. The numerous landing piers still exist, but the queues of cars have gone. Still, there is heavy traffic and more will be coming in the near future with the new light railway to Karaköy under construction and the extension of the underground line from Taksim to Fındıklı.

Nevertheless there are architectural features of rank in the area. This is – in the first place – the Fındıklı camii/Molla Çelebi camii, a work of the famous Ottoman architect Sinan, dating from 1589 or 1565/66 (MÜLLER-WIENER 1977, p. 413). There was once a little külliye, a medrese and a hamam, but the hamam was removed in 1958 when the main street was widened to a coastal thoroughfare (MÜLLER-WIENER 1977, p. 413).

Up on the slope is the Cihangir mosque, dating from 1890, built by Abdülhamit II. (1876-1909) on the site of an earlier mosque by Sinan which burned down in 1720 (SUMNER-BOYD & FREELY 1972, p. 468). Cihangir was the hunchback son of Süleyman the Magnificent (1520-1566) who died in 1530. Besides, there are fountains near the coastal thoroughfare, the Hakimoğlu Ali Paşa çeşmesi and the fountain of Koca Yusuf Paşa, who was Grand Vezir to Abdülhamit I. (1774-1789) (SUMNER-BOYD & FREELY 1972, p. 469).

Presently the tertiary sector of the mega city Istanbul is expanding rapidly and this means it does not only expand into the Tophane section with offices related to shipping (Deniz Ticaret Odası, Deniz Yolları İşletmesi, Salıpazarı Gümrük Depoları, Ulaştırma Bakanlığı Istanbul Bölge Müdürlüğü) but also into the Fındıklı-Kabataş section.

The most prominent representative of the tertiary sector is the Mimar Sinan Üniversitesi at the water's edge. This is not detrimental, but rather typical of the Bosphorus sea- and landscape, its seaside being lined and graced with a wide range of educational features of the tertiary sector.

5.5 The Dolmabahçe Section

This is one of the top-ranking assets of the Bosphorus sea- and landscape: a large palace with a 300 m facade on the Bosphorus, a mosque (Dolmabahçe camii) and a clock tower

(Dolmabahçe Saat Kulesi) all lined up at the water's edge, directly at the sea. All three date back to the same period, the second half of the 19th century.

It was the time of reform in the Ottoman Empire – or what was left of it. Mahmut II. (1808/1839) and Abdülmecit II. (1839-1861) were reforming sultans endeavouring to reduce the political and military drawbacks of the Ottoman state by leaving old traditions behind and turning to westernization (HELLIER & VENTURI 1994, pp. 151-182).

The change of headgear at the time of Mahmut II. from turban to fez is symbolic. There was a strong French influence in many respects, not the least in architecture. Leaving old traditions behind resulted in the exodus of the ruling Ottoman family from the Topkapı Sarayı into a new residence on the Bosphorus – the Dolmabahçe Sarayı.

This palace, built on reclaimed land where once had been a small bay of the Bosphorus, had forerunners in the form of a summer residence of the ruling Ottoman family, a pavilion (Turkish: köşk) or wooden palace since the 16th century (TUCHELT 1962, p. 174), setting early the fashion of building summer houses (Turkish sing.: yalı) on the Bosphorus – a fashion that spread slowly in the course of history from the ruling family to the wealthy and has today reached comparatively ordinary people.

The present Dolmabahçe Sarayı was built from 1844 to 1853 and opened in 1856 (GÜLERSOY 1973, pp. 242-269) – the delay caused by the Crimean War (1853-1856) – after the so-called summer palace of Beşiktaş (TUCHELT 1962, p. 175), the immediate forerunner in Selim III. (1789-1807) time, had been pulled down. The architects were Nikoğos and Karabet Balyan, two members of the Balyan family of architects, and the palace was built in an opulent neo-baroque style with abounding decorations outside and inside – at a time when the Ottoman state was already in dire financial circumstances (SUMNER-BOYD & FREELY 1972, p. 470). A detailed description of the posh interior is given by GÜLERSOY (1973, pp. 242-269), an architectural evaluation by HELLIER & VENTURI (1994, pp 151-172; cp. YERASIMOS 2000, pp. 361-366).

Within the Topkapı Sarayı several mosques existed for the ruling Ottoman family to fulfil their religious obligations, but there was and is no mosque inside the Dolmabahçe – an influence of westernization? So a separate mosque was built, the Dolmabahçe camii, a little distance away, at the water's edge (SUMNER-BOYD & FREELY 1972, p. 470). The building was begun by Bezmialem Valide Sultan, the mother of Abdülmecit I. (1839-1861) and finished in 1853 – the same time as the Dolmabahçe palace. The style of the mosque, for which Nikoğos Balyan was responsible, met with criticism from modern architects (SUMNER-BOYD & FREELY 1972, p. 470).

Only a little later, in 1894, a clock tower completed the Dolmabahçe trinity of architectural modernism in the second half of the 19th century (KREISER 2001, p. 181). The mania of building clock towers at the time – the Dolmabahçe one is with 30 m the tallest – is symbolic of modernism in the late Ottoman period. Few people being in the possession of a watch general information about hours and minutes was available for everybody now and the European time scale was introduced beside the traditional alla-turca-time scale (KREISER 2001, p.181; GOODWIN 1971, p. 419).

The Tophane section suffered from the incurrence of the tertiary sector, concealing today the architectural splendours of the past from the Bosphorus. Luckily this is not the case in the Dolmabahçe section – though the tertiary sector moved in heavily. The physical background of the sea front, the steep slopes, are today massively occupied by hotels. The first large international hotel after the Second World War was the Hilton, the latest ones are the tall hotel towers of the Ritz Carlton and the less eye-catching Swiss-otel The Bosphorus, but the municipality gas tank, which disgraced part of the slope, is gone. And there are other hotels, partly out of sight from the Bosphorus, the Divan, the Hyatt Regency and the Ceylan Inter-Continental. The Inönü Football Stadium, on level ground and therefore not too conspicuous, is however an extremely contrasting neighbour to the Dolmabahçe palace.

But the architecturally graceful lines of the hotels behind the Dolmabahçe Sarayı do not impair the attractions of the area as a highlight of the Bosphorus sea- and landscape.

5.6 The Beşiktaş Section

On the western side of the lower Bosphorus ancient and modern monuments have to compete in prominence in several sections with the land uses of the tertiary sector in the form of traffic – sea and land traffic – offices and hotels for tourism. The Beşiktaş section is such an area with heavy traffic and other features of the tertiary sector, but important ancient monuments are embedded.

The Barbaros Bulvarı, a wide boulevard, constructed in the 1960ties (LEITNER 1965, p. 51) for the adjustment of the city of Istanbul to the motorcar, to connect the inner urban area with the new development region of the four Levent settlements and beyond (LEITNER 1971, pp. 58, 59, 67), branches off from the coastal road, goes up the gentle hill, leads also – today – to the first bridge across the Bosphorus, and produces leavy traffic for the Beşiktaş landing jetties, which are surrounded by pleasant little parks.

An ancient monument of architectural importance is the Sinan Paşa camii, at the corner where the Barbaros Bulvarı joins the coastal road. This mosque (MÜLLER-WIENER 1977, p. 459 – with groundplan; cp. GOODWIN 1971, p. 244 – with groundplan) was built by Sinan, the most famous of Ottoman architects,before 1533 and completed with a medrese, a hamam and a türbe. It was founded for the brother of the Vezir Rüstem Paşa, the Kapudanpaşa Sinanpaşa, who died in 1533. The mosque is a copy of the Üç Şerefli camii from 1447 at Edirne (SUMNER-BOYD & FREELY 1972, p. 479). Nearby, in one of the parks at the seaside, is the mausoleum/türbe of the most famous of Ottoman sea heroes, the great pirate admiral Hayrettin Paşa, called Barbaros, who died in 1546 (SUMNER-BOYD & FREELY 1972, p. 479). It is an octagonal structure and one of the earliest works of Sinan. Not far from it is a statue of Barbaros.

This assembly is surrounded by museums, the Deniz Müzesi (English: Naval Museum), with ancient stately rowing-boats of the Ottoman sultans used for the processions from the Topkapı Sarayı to the summer residences on the Bosphorus, and there is the Resin ve Heykel Müzesi (English: Museum of Fine Arts). Some schools and offices follow on the seaside, all of little architectural importance.

As a mixture of old and new, functional and pittoresque, the Beşiktaş section is in a limited way a contribution to the beauty of the Bosphorus sea- and landscape.

5.7 The Çırağan-Yıldız Section

Two, in size and structure different sub-areas make up the Çırağan-Yıldız section: one is the Çırağan Sarayı, immediately at the water's edge, a companion piece to the Dolmabahçe Sarayı, the other is the very large Yıldız Parkı with an assembly of different buildings, palaces and pavilions, on the gentle slope behind the Çırağan palace, reaching up almost to the Barbaros Bulvarı. The bridge across the coastal road behind the Çırağan palace, which originally connected the palace and the park, still exists.

A passenger on a Bosphorus ferry passing along gets no glimpse of the park but is the more impressed by the water front of the palace in all its splendours. The (old) Çırağan palace burned down in 1910, remained a ruin for eighty years, was taken over in 1991 by the Kempinski hotel group (GORYS 2003, pp. 163, 98) and had its outside restored and the inside changed into the top luxury hotel of the city of Istanbul.

Most of the Yıldız Parkı has been turned into an elegant public recreation ground with excellent restoration of several buildings done by the Turkish Touring and Automobile Club (Turkish: Türkiye Turing ve Otomobil Kurumu) under the leadership of its late Director-General Çelik Gülersoy (STEWIG 1986, pp. 64-66).

The Çırağan palace had – like the Dolmabahçe palace, the exterior of which looks a little neglected compared to the Çırağan palace – its forerunners. On its site existed since the early 18th century (1721) at least a pavilion or a small garden palace – typical of the early sporadic suburbanization on the Bosphorus of high ranking officials (TUCHELT 1962, pp. 174-177; HELLIER & VENTURI 1994, pp. 185-194; GÜLERSOY 1973, p. 270).

After the forerunner buildings had been pulled down Mahmut II. (1808-1831) had a new Çırağan palace built in 1836-1839 (TUCHELT 1962, p. 176), but construction continued until 1874 under Sultan Abdülaziz (1861-1871) (SUMNER-BOYD & FREELY 1972, p. 480; HELLIER & VENTURI 1994, pp. 184-194). Again one of the Balyan family of architects, Nikoğos, styled the palace after European models with – desired by Sultan Abdülaziz – an Arabian touch (HELLIER & VENTURI 1994, p. 185; YERASIMOS 2000, pp. 372-374). It is the palace in which the Çırağan incident happened in 1878 – a conspiracy that failed, trying to get Murat V. (1876), who had become sultan is 1876 and was deposed the same year, back on the throne (KREISER 2001, pp. 228-229; HELLIER & VENTURI 1994, p. 191).

In the Yıldız Parkı, the other, very large area of the section the number and variety of the buildings, palaces and pavilions, is surprising: the Yıldız Sarayı at the highest point of the park, not far from the Barbaros Bulvarı, the Küçük and Büyük Mabeyn for the seperation of private and official rooms, the Şale Köşkü, the Malta Köşkü, the Çadır Köşkü; there is a mosque, the Yıldız camii (YERASIMOS 2000, p. 374) and there is even a porcelain manufactury (Turkish: Yıldız Çinive Porselen Sanayi Işletmesi) (HELLIER & VENTURI 1994, pp. 201-219). The construction extended over a long period, the second half of the 19th century during the long reign of Abdülhamit II. (1876-1909) and the buildings were often remodelled.

The term pavilion is – in several cases – an understatement: the fifty rooms of the Şale Köşkü are compatible with a palace and its architecture of a Swiss chalet is typical of the variety of styles (HELLIER & VENTURI 1994, pp. 201, 206). Of the Balyan family of architects the brothers Sarkis and Simon drafted the earlier pavilions; an Italian architect, Raimondo D'Aronco, worked on the later and contributed to the architectural variety of Victorian inns, alpine huts and Italian style villas (HELLIER & VENTURI 1994, p. 200).

Abdülhamit II. (1876-1909) – a sultan afraid of assassinations and with a deviant behaviour – spent almost the complete time of his long reign within the Yıldız park and its buildings (HELLIER & VENTURI 1994, p. 201). He had a private zoo installed in the park.

As it was the case with both, the Dolmabahçe and the Çırağan Sarayı – no mosque inside to perform the religious duties – Abdülhamit II. (1876-1909) had the Hamidiye camii built in 1886, near the southern entrance to the park, opposite the Çırağan palace (HELLIER & VENTURI 1994, p. 210). There, another little mosque, of wood and older, dating from 1570, is nearby, the Yahya Efendi camii with a medrese and a türbe, a small külliye, the work of Sinan (SUMNER-BOYD & FREELY 1972, pp. 481, 535). Yahya Efendi was a foster-brother of Süleyman the Magnificent (1520-1566).

The preservation of the large area of the Yıldız park prevented the mass invasion of the tertiary sector into the Çırağan-Yıldız section. However, the Yıldız Technical University got hold of the northwestern fringe of the Yıldız park and some related offices installed themselves there too, like the Chamber of Engineers and Architects (Turkish: Mühendis ve Mimar Odaları Birliği). A large modern hotel, the Conrad, also stands on the western fringe, at the Barbaros Bulvarı.

In all, the restored Çırağan palace (-hotel, hotel-palace) at the water front is the jewel of the section, but the restored palaces and pavilions are no lesser ornaments and – though not directly facing the Bosphorus – can not be excluded. The Çırağan section is without doubt one of the highlights of the Bosphorus sea- and landscape.

5.8 The Ortaköy Section

Though Ortaköy belongs to the lower Bosphorus region and though Ortaköy is not too far away from the oldest quarters of the city of Istanbul the settlement originates – as part of its name, - köy, implies – from a village. Probably fishing was the dominant occupation of the villagers. The strong currents of the narrow section of the Bosphorus rush past the settlement, the traditional fishing grounds extend on the opposite side of the coast in calmer water (LEITNER 1971, p. 63 – map).

Ortaköy is a mixture of not too old and very modern. The most favourable impression is that of the Ortaköy camii, at the water's edge – once more a contribution to the gracefulness of the Bosphorus sea- and landscape. The mosque, dating from 1854, on the site of an earlier mosque, was built at the time of Abdülmecit I. (1839-1861) by Nikoğos Balyan, a member of the great family of architects, in a mixed style (SUMNER-BOYD & FREELY 1972, p. 483).

There is an ancient bath house, built by Sinan, the Hüsrev Küthüda hamamı, hidden from the Bosphorus, in a row of houses, at the high street of the settlement (SUMNER-BOYD & FREELY 1972, p. 482/483).

Ortaköy was chosen by several second-rank Ottoman officials, ministers of the Ottoman government, for large and small summer residences (Turkish sing.: yalı) (MEYER 1908, p. 300), one of which is a charming ruin, the Esma Sultan palace (HINKLE & SLUIS 2003, p. 24).
The mosque, together with the landing jetty and the restaurants, which have made the seaside a fashionable meeting place for young people, is a pittoresque sight. With the heavy international shipping traffic to be observed on the water and the suspension bridge across the Bosphorus with its very high pylon (165 m) standing nearby the sight is full of tension between the old and the new.

This bridge, the Avrupa Köprüsü (also Boğaziçi Köprüsü), the first across the Bosphorus which was opened in 1973 on occasion of the 50th anniversary of the Republic of Turkey, serves as a contrasting and peculiar setting for Ortaköy (SUMNER-BOYD & FREELY 1972, p. 483). The bridge road runs in a clear height of 64 meters not only across the Bosphorus but also across Ortaköy – with a continuous day and night flow of heavy traffic and consequently noise.

There had been discussions about the style of the bridge. Before the present bridge was built it was advocated by the German town planner of Istanbul (HÖGG 1967, p. 328), to construct a low bridge of reinforced concrete – allegedly for aesthetic reasons – with several short and clumsy pillars and with a clear height of only 50 meters – insufficient for tall ships to pass underneath.

Luckily this type of bridge was not built. The present bridge with its graceful, extremely slender horizontal and vertical lines in no way diminuates the aesthetic impression of the Bosphorus sea- and landscape. This applies also to the second suspension bridge, the Fatih Sultan Mehmet Köprüsü of 1988, a copy of the first, a distance farther north.
Latest development is the appearance of international hotels, as the spearhead of the hotel agglomeration of the Dolmabahçe and Çırağan sections, in the form of the Radison SAS Bosphorus. But the Ortaköy section graces the Bosphorus sea- and landscape with its recreational and pittoresque elements.

5.9 The Kuruçeşme-Arnavutköy-Bebek Section

When the Ottoman ruling family decided to have palaces and parks outside the Topkapı Sarayı their first orientation was the upper Golden Horn, the valleys of the Alibeyköy and Kağıthane rivers, where Ahmet III. (1703-1730) ordered, in 1721 and 1722, the two garden palaces of Chosrewabad and Beharabad to be built (TUCHELT 1962, p. 170). But the interest also turned towards both sides of the Bosphorus – the present Dolmabahçe, Çırağan and Beylerbeyi palaces had several predecessors. Even beyond the lower Bosphorus the Ottoman ruling family reached out with their garden palaces.

The palace Neşatabad and a large park was built by the Hatice Sultan at Defterdarburnu – that is at the southern tip of Kuruçeşme – and the palace Humayunabad, also with a large park, was built at Bebek (TUCHELT1962 pp. 171, 172). Both are gone without trace. On the map of the Bosphorus drawn by von MOLTKE (1893) the Mirimah Sultan Sarayı is still in its place near the cape of Akıntı Burnu, where the current of the Bosphorus is the fiercest (SUMNER-BOYD & FREELY 1972, p. 485).

Presently the Princess Naila mansion, which originally belonged to one of the daughters of Abdülhamit II. (1876-1909), a little up the hill in a forest preserve, is a reminder of the past (HINKLE & SLUIS 2003, p. 27).

What a contrast to modern times! When the city authorities of Istanbul looked for urgently needed quay space for the expansion of the port of Istanbul they decided to make Kuruçeşme – from 1955 on – the quay for handling bulk cargo (Turkish: Kömür Parkı) (LEITNER 1967, p. 35), mainly coal from the Turkish Zonguldak coalfields on the Black Sea coast.

It has to be admitted this disfigured the water front and was very detrimental to the beauty of the Bosphorus sea- and landscape (SUMNER-BOYD & FREELY 1972, p. 484). But luckily, another fundamental change of land use happened in 1968: Kuruçeşme (which means: dry spring), the coal quay of the port of Istanbul, was given up and the area refigured as a coastal park with a marina, which adds to the beauty of the Bosphorus sea- and landscape. This is one of the examples of intentional planning of the city authorities for the better – contributing, together with other examples, still to be mentioned, systematically to the enhancement of the beauty of the Bosphorus sea- and landscape.

Once the Ottoman ruling family had settled in an area – at least in the summer months – high ranking officials, Levantine businesmen and rich members of the non-Muslim community/minority followed. Arnavutköy and Bebek, originally villages of fishermen and mariners, became favourable sites for summer residences, yalılar (Turkish plural of yalı) and houses (Turkish plural: hanelar). The yalılar were mostly in the possession of Muslims, the hanelar in the possession of Christians and Jews, but were not necessarily minor summer residences (but compare HINKLE & SLUIS 2003, p. 41). In a list, translated from the original sources, KREISER (2001, p. 222 – table) mentions for Arnavutköy and (Küçük) Bebek, i. e. on both flanks of Akıntı Burnu, for 1815 17 yalılar and 17 hanelar (16 Christians, 1 Jew) and gives details about the social ranks of the proprietors.

They were the predecessors of what exists today on the water front of Arnavutköy and Bebek – not as high-brow as before, but still with well-liked Mediterranean urban flair (SUMNER-BOYD & FREELY 1972, pp. 484, 486).

Not far from a little mosque, the Bebek camii, which dates from 1913 and was styled by Kemalettin Bey, a leader of the neo-classical school of Turkish architecture (SUMNER-BOYD & FREELY 1972, p. 486), is a reminiscence of the (old) summer residences, the Egyptian consulate (HINKLE & SLUIS 2003, p. 31).

Originally this was the summer residence of the last viceroy of Egypt, Abbas Hilmi II., who had his palace, the Hidiv Kasrı in Kanlıca, near Çubuklu, on the other side of the Bosphorus. When in 1914 Egypt became a British protectorate, the yalı was made the seat of the Egyptian ambassador to the Sublime Porte – as long as Istanbul remained the capital city of the Ottoman state. But that wasn't long. When Ankara took over Istanbul's function as capital city the yalı was down-graded to consulate (HELLIER & VENTURI 1994, p. 134). This summer residence was fashioned in the decorative style of around 1900 (German: Jugendstil; Italian: stile floreale), nicely screened from the Bosphorus by a grilled fence, but inside the traditional division into Haremlik and Selamlık remained (HELLIER & VENTURI 1994, p. 134).

Above Arnavutköy a small area may be found on a map bearing the name of Robert Koleji. This was originally the American College for Girls, founded in 1871, only a few years after the Robert College from 1863, a few miles to the north, the forerunner of what is today – and since 1971 – the Boğaziçi Üniversitesi (SUMNER-BOYD & FREELY 1972, p. 485-487). On occasion of the centenial of the co-educational American College for Girls it took on – in 1971, when the original Robert College became the Bosphorus University – the name of Robert College.

In the Kuruçeşme-Arnavutköy-Bebek section now all three, Kuruçeşme, Arnavutköy and Bebek are the attractions, fashionable meeting places and little resorts, which contribute with their Mediterranean charm to the beauty of the Bosphorus sea- and landscape.

5.10 The Rumeli Hisarı Section

This is an other top quality historical and cultural feature of the Bosphorus sea- and landscape: a late medieval castle on the Bosphorus, its western side, opposite the corresponding castle on the eastern side of a little earlier time, the Anadolu Hisarı.

The conqueror of Constantinople, Sultan Mehmet II. (1451-1481) had the castle built in 1452, a year before the siege began (MÜLLER-WIENER 1977, p. 335; GOODWIN 1991, p. 103). The castle's function was – together with that of the opposite Anadolu Hisarı – to close the Bosphorus as a sea lane to cut off possible supplies for Constantinople which was conquered in 1453.

The construction encouraged an enormous effort; 3000 workers were employed; it took only four months to complete the castle (MÜLLER-WIENER 1977, p. 335 – ground plan on p. 336; GOODWIN 1991 – ground plan on p. 103; KREISER 2001 – ground plan on p. 217).

The fortress is about 250 m in length and about 120 m in width (MÜLLER-WIENER 1977, p. 335). It has been evaluated by GOODWIN (1991, p. 104) as of an international type, which relied much an contemporaneous and earlier castles in southeastern Anatolia (Diyarbakır) and Syria (Kraks of the Crusaders).

It has three large towers, one in the north, a little inland on the upper slope, the Black Tower (Turkish: Karaküle), the second, also on the upper slope a little to the south, the Rose Tower (Türkish: Gülküle) and the third, originally at the water's edge. The round towers – with a diameter between 23,8 and 26,7 meters – were constructed under the auspices of Sultan Mehmet II. vezirs: Saruça Paşa (the north tower), Zaganos (the south tower) and Çandarlı Habil Paşa (the tower at the water) (MÜLLER-WIENER 1977, p. 335; GOODWIN 1991, p. 104).

The two inland and upper towers stand opposite each other and are connected by a wall, up to 7 meters thick, across a little valley in which a subterranean little river flows to the

Bosphorus. There are gates, smaller towers between the large ones and a barbican. Within the castle area were – originally – billets for the soldiers, the Janissaries, the elite corps of Ottoman soldiers, a bath house and a mosque with a minaret.

After the conquest of Constantinople and the expansion of the Ottoman Empire in southern Russia – making the Black Sea an inland lake – the castle became useless and decayed (MÜLLER-WIENER 1977, p. 357).

In 1940/41 a coastal road was constructed between Rumeli Hisarı and the sea (MÜLLER-WIENER 1977, p. 357). However, in 1953, on occasion of the 500th anniversary of the conquest of Constantinople the castle was splendidly restored, the houses inside removed and the interior prepared for the celebration of festivals – summer productions of Shakespeare (GORYS 2003, p. 170; SUMNER-BOYD & FREELY 1972, p. 489) – with grand views of the Bosphorus sea- and landscape.

Above the slope of Rumeli Hisarı is the large precinct of the Boğaziçi Üniversitesi, the Bosphorus University, established in 1971 on the grounds of the formerly American Robert College, the section for boys, founded in 1863 – an institution of learning which produced many scholars, scientists and literary men in and for Turkey (SUMNER-BOYD & FREELY 1972, pp. 486/487).

There are in the Rumeli Hisarı village several mosques, near the water, which – like the Ali Pertek camii – may be classed as neighbourhood mosques of little architectural importance. One however, the Kemalettin camii, built just before the First World War in 1913, is remarkable because of its Ottoman Renaissance, nationalistic style (YERASIMOS 2000, p. 377).

The second great suspension bridge across the Bosphorus, the Fatih Sultan Mehmet Köprüsü, opened in 1988 to relief the enormous motor traffic of the Istanbul region, closes the Rumeli Hisarı section in the north. It has already been stated that – in construction details a copy of the first bridge – its extremely slender vertical and horizontal lines are in no way detrimental to the beauty of the Bosphorus sea- and landscape.

5.11 The Emirgan-Istinye Section

In the Kuruçeşme sub-section an extraordinary contrast existed – for some time in the recent past – between the original early Ottoman land use by a palace and a park and the land use as coal port. There was – also for some time in the recent past – a similar extraordinary contrast between the Istinye and Emirgan sub-sections.

Istinye is a bay, narrow compared to the wide bays of Büyükdere or Beykoz. This topography made Istinye a harbour, well protected from winds of all directions, specially the strong northeastern and southwestern winds (Turkish: poyraz and lodos). This is probably the reason for Istinye becoming a naval base. Aerial photos exist, taken from an airship in 1916 (LANGENSIEPEN & GÜLERYÜZ 1995, p. 132), showing the ex-German battle-cruiser Yavuz (ex Goeben) and the ex-German cruiser Midilli (ex Breslau) at Istinye, beside a floating dock. The shipyard and the floating docks, which existed since 1907(LEITNER 1971, p. 61), together with some small industrial firms (LEITNER 1971, p. 61; TÜMER-TEKIN 1974-1976, pp. 2, 15-22) dominated the southern side of Istinye bay. But in 1992 the shipyard, the floating dock and the industrial firms came to an end (HINKLE & SLUIS 2003, p. 39). This is another excellent example of land use change with the intension of enhancing the beauty of the Bosphorus sea- and landscape – on its western side. Istinye bay is now a fashionable marina bordering the Emirgan park (Turkish: Emirgan Korusu).

The village and park of Emirgan take its name from a Persian prince, Emirgune, who is supposed to have rendered the city of Erivan to Sultan Murat IV. (1623-1640) without attack and was rewarded with a palace and a park near the village of Emirgan (SUMNER-BOYD & FREELY 1972, p. 489/490).

The palace is gone, but the park remained and blossomed. The pavilions (Turkish sing.: köşk) exist on the slopes of the park, the Pink Pavilion (Turkish: Pembe Köşk), the Yellow Pavilion (Turkish: Sarı Köşk) and the White Pavilion (Turkish: Beyaz Köşk). It was the late Director-General of the Turkish Automobile Club (Turkish: Türkiye Turing ve Otomobil Kurumu) Çelik Gülersoy, who was responsible for the splendid restoration work (STEWIG 1986, p. 66).

The park is a favourite of garden lovers; there is a special concern for the cultivation of flowers including the many varieties of the tulip, the endogenous Ottoman flower (GORYS 2003, p. 170), name-giving to the Tulip Period (1718-1730). There is also a museum with paintings and calligraphies in the so-called Horse Pavilion (Turkish: Atlı Köşk) (GORYS 2003, p. 170).

The situation of Emirgan on the Bosphorus attracted visitors, tourists and residential population since a long time. Beside a baroque mosque, the Emirgan camii, partly of wood, built by Sultan Abdülhamit I. (1774-1789) in 1781/82 (SUMNER-BOYD & FREELY 1972, p. 490), is an ancient yalı, perhaps partly going back to Emirgune's time (SUMNER-BOYD & FREELY 1972, p. 490). It is the Şerifler yalı, named after a Şerif of Mecca, Abdullah Paşa, who was one of the many proprietors (HELLIER & VENTURI 1994, pp. 112, 117; HINKLE & SLUIS 2003, p. 38).

The rather plain and rustic style of the exterior, which had to endure alterations in the 18th century, contrasts with the opulent interior. Only the Selamlık still exists with its traditional ground plan. Some visitors observed a disharmony of style between the baroque decorations and the relatively modern European furniture (HELLIER & VENTURI 1994, p. 117). The yalı has been restored in the eighties (HELLIER & VENTURI 1994, p. 147).

The Emirgan-Istinye Section is nowadays a continuous, uninterrupted addition to the beauty of the Bosphorus sea- and landscape.

5.12 The Yeniköy-Tarabya Section

When the scale of social ranking is applied to this section both sub-sections, the Yeniköy as well as the Tarabya sub-section, occupy the upper ranks. This structure developed without the Ottoman ruling family having palaces or parks built in the area which seemed to be too far away from their sites on the lower Bosphorus.

The social quality of the residential population north and south of the little bay of Tarabya and also in the Yeniköy part, just round the bay of Istinye, has to do with the shoreline being selected in the 18th/19th centuries by rich families of the Greek minority in Istanbul and rich Turkish families for summer residences (MEYER 1908, pp. 301-303; BAEDEKER 1914, pp. 230/231). Is seems that the non-Muslims settled north and south of the bay of Tarabya, the Muslims preferred Yeniköy. Typical of the early fashionable quality of the area is the once existence of the expensive hotel Tokatlian, at the water's edge, on the corner of the entrance to the bay of Tarabya (MEYER 1908, p. 302; BAEDEKER 1914, p. 231; MAMBOURY 1930, p. 181).

The elevated social position of the area was emphasized when the residential population partly changed. Mainly in the Tarabya sub-section, north and south of the little bay of Tarabya, a new type of summer residences was created.

As long as Istanbul remained the political centre and capital city of the Ottoman state the foreign political powers were represented at the Sublime Porte by ambassadors who resided in the old quarters of the city of Istanbul, in Beyoğlu, north of the Golden Horn.

The Tarabya section, north and south of the bay of Tarabya, was selected for the summer residences with large gardens or parks by the ambassadors and used as such even after the function of capital city had moved from Istanbul to Ankara in 1923.

So there is from south to north a series of high ranking villas, surrounded by gardens and parks, which were the summer residences of the ambassadors of Austria and Germany (south of the bay of Tarabya) and Italy, France and Britain (north of the bay of Tarabya) (MEYER 1908, p. 302; BAEDEKER 1914, p. 230; SUMNER-BOYD & FREELY 1972, p. 491; HINKLE & SLUIS 2003, pp. 42, 47-51; IREZ & AKSU 1992). Near the German residence is a war cemetery with the graves of (high ranking) soldiers, who lost their lives during the First World War in service with the Ottoman army and navy (GORYS 2003, p. 170).

The bay of Tarabya was used by stationary warships that were at the disposal of the ambassadors (MEYER 1908, p. 302). Today the bay of Tarabya is a posh marina and at the entrance to the bay stands – in the place of its predecessor Tokatlian – the expensive modern hotel Tarabya, at the water's edge. In May 2006 it was being renovated.

There are quite a number of partly ancient summer residences (Turkish plural: yalılar) of Turkish proprietors. On the coast road of Yeniköy even a bus stop is named Yalılar. Foreign and Christian subjects of the non-Muslim minorities had settled in Yeniköy also – according to the number of still existing churches, a little away from the water's edge (Meryem Ana Ermeni Kilisesi, Aya Nikola Rum Kilisesi, Panayia Rum Kilisesi).

The best known yalılar are these: the Sait Halim Paşa yalısı, the Afif Paşa yalısı. The favourite situation for the yalılar is the fact that the coastal road runs a little away from the Bosphorus so that the yalılar have direct admission to the water. The four storey high Afif Paşa yalısı is a mixture of architectural styles, belonging to the so-called cosmopolitan period (1867-1908) (HELLIER & VENTURI 1994, p. 138; HINKLE & SLUIS 2003, p. 40).

There are also elegant and fashionable yalılar standing in a row, undetached, without gardens, immediately at the waters's edge (HELLIER & VENTURI 1994, p. 138). Sait Halim Paşa was an Egyptian prince and Grand Vezir. His yalı is a stately mansion with a special quay at the Bosphorus, gardens on two sides and a park behind which once could be reached by means of a bridge across the coastal road (HELLIER & VENTURI 1994, p. 122; HINKLE & SLUIS 2004, p. 45).

Outside and inside the style is that of eclecticism typical of the so-called cosmopolitic period, a mixture of Oriental and Occidental elements, but with Selamlık on the ground floor and Haremlik on the first floor. The various rooms were reserved for a certain style each. On the whole, French influence dominated and even statues of undressed women can be found. Besides the European style Egyptian and Ottoman stylish elements are present (HELLIER & VENTURI 1994, pp. 122-123, 129).

Other yalıs from Yeniköy to Tarabya shall only be mentioned. They are pictured and briefly characterized by HINKLE & SLUIS, 2003, pp. 42-48: from south to north Çaycı Istapan yalı, Faruk Sezerar yalı, Üstünkaya yalı, Rasim Ferit Bey yalı, Şehzade Burhanettim Efendi yalı, Gazioğlu yalı, Bayazcıyan yalı, Kara Todori yalı, Mısırlı Fuat Bey yalı, Feridun yalı, Twin yalı, Ali Rıza Paşa yalı, Muvaffak Gönen yalı, Dadyan yalı, Sandoz yalı, Kalkavan yalı.

Together with the high-priced coffee-houses, restaurants, hotels and marinas the lavish arrangement of the many types of mostly elegant summer residences the Yeniköy-Tarabya section is an admirable contribution to the Bosphorus sea- and landscape.

5.13 The Büyükdere-Sariyer Section

This section is characterised by its wide bay, off the main traffic route of Bosphorus transit shipping. The bay was used – before the Second World War – as the seaplane airport of Istanbul with connections to Athens, Brindisi and Rhodes (MAMBOURY 1930, p. 184).

Büyükdere (English: great valley) is the entrance valley to the interior and the Belgrade Forest with its reservoirs (Turkish sing.: bend) for the water supply of the city of Istanbul (SUMNER-BOYD & FREELY 1972, p. 492).

The rising landscape in the north protects Sariyer and part of Büyükdere from strong and cold northerly winds, so that the fishing villages had a chance of becoming little resorts and sites of summer residences of people who wish to avoid these strong winds at certain times of the year (MEYER 1908, p. 303). The summer residences of the diplomats of Russia and Spain are also to be found there (SUMNER-BOYD & FREELY 1972, p. 491; HINKLE & SLUIS 2003, pp. 52-54).

A limited number of stately yalıs exist: The Fuat Paşa yalı, the Koçataş yalı, the Balaban yalı (HINKLE & SLUIS 2003, p. 52). The Azaryan yalı, splendidly restored by the Veh-bi Koç Foundation (Turkish: Vakfı) is being used by the Sandberk Hanım Museum of Art and Antiquities (HINKLE & SLUIS 2003, p. 55).

The entrance valley to the interior is fertile, so horticultural land use with a food market in the near city of Istanbul is prevalent (LEITNER 1971, p. 67 – map). Sariyer is also a fish market, the closest outlet for the Black Sea fisheries (SUMNER-BOYD & FREELY 1972, p. 493). The surroundings of Büyükdere suffered a little from unplanned suburbanization of industry (LEITNER 1971, p. 61; TÜMERTEKIN 1974-1976, pp. 2, 22-27). In that Büyükdere is a counter part to Paşabahçe – Beykoz on the opposite side of the Bosphorus, but to a smaller extent. However, there was a time when the mostly small industrial firms attracted gecekondu evler in the neighbourhood (TÜMERTEKIN 1974-1976, pp. 16-18).

On the whole the residential and touristic population of the Büyükdere-Sariyer section occupies the middle ranks of the social ladder. The area is not unattractive but it lacks the outstanding splendours of other sections of the Bosphorus sea- and landscape.

5.14 The Rumeli Kavağı Section

On the western side of the Bosporus the last stop of the excursion ferries on their northern route is Rumeli Kavağı. Originally a fishing village the settlement developed into a little resort although the (day-) excursion ferries cross the Bosphorus to Anadolu Kavağı for the lunch-time stop-over. North of Rumeli Kavağı the rugged coastline with steep cliffs and almost purely natural scenes begins and reaches to the northern entrance of the Bosphorus.

There are very scanty ruins of an ancient castle above the village, up on the peneplain. They mark the strategic position of Rumeli Kavağı as sentinel of the northern entrance to the Bosphorus. The castle originated in Byzantine times, was later taken over by the Genoese and still later by the Ottomans, who are supposed to have built a wall, down the steep slope, and fastened a chain across the Bosphorus to the corresponding castle of Anadolu Kavağı on the other side to close the sea lane against attacks and for shipping (MEYER 1908, pp. 306-307).

The pressure exercised by the Russian southward advance in the Black Sea since the 17th century (KREISER 2001, p. 71) induced the Sultans Abdülhamit I. (1774-1789) and Selim III. (1789-1807) to order French military engineers, Baron Le Tott,Toussaint in 1783 and Monnier in 1799, to place batteries in defensive positions around Rumeli Kavağı – just as on the other, eastern side of the Bosphorus around Anadolu Kavağı (SUMNER-BOYD & FREELY 1972, p. 495; cp. von MOLTKE 1893, map of the Bosphorus; HINKLE & SLUIS 2003, p. 57).

Together with the parallel naming of Rumeli Hisarı and Anadolu Hisarı the couple of Rumeli Kavağı and Anadolu Kavağı clearly indicate the grid lay-out of cultural institutions as the fundamental structure of the Bosphorus sea- and landscape.

5.15 The Haydarpaşa-Harem Section

This area is the Anatolian side of the southern entrance to the Bosphorus, a small coastal plain with level ground, closed inland in the north by steep slopes which – in the geological past – had been active sea cliffs, eroded by waves driven by strong lodos winds.

The area is dominated by traffic and traffic installations, stretching from Haydarpaşa to Harem in the north, but there are several large buildings which – in different ways – characterize the sea front and the skyline of this section visually. In the south – outside the area – is Kadıköy, the site of the ancient Greek colony Calchedon, which was founded in 680 B.C., twenty years before Byzantion in the west (MERLE 1916, p. 86); but no remains exist.

Leaving out of consideration the several small harbours on the Marmara and Golden Horn coasts of Byzantion (MÜLLER-WIENER 1994), the port of Istanbul was – for a long time, until the 19th/20th centuries – the Golden Horn, a real harbour, offering protection from winds and gales from all sides (MÜLLER-WIENER 1994). But with the increase in the volume of shipping traffic, the growth of the size of ships and the coming of railways to the Ottoman state, the port of Istanbul – as far as cargo is concerned–moved to the Anatolian side of the southern entrance to the Bosphorus (ETHEM 1929; LEITNER 1965, 1967).

The first port installations at Haydarpaşa date back to the construction of the railway line from Izmit to Haydarpaşa in 1870/72, together with a small railway station, the forerunner of the present arrangement (MÜLLER-WIENER 1994, p. 123). It was the Anatolian (and Bagdad) Railway built for German interests since 1888 that made Haydarpaşa the great railway arrival point from the interior of Anatolia which caused the enlargement of port facilities. The present impressive station building – itself a piece of history, but in full use – was erected from 1905 to 1909 (MÜLLER-WIENER 1994, p. 224). The new port had already been opened in 1903. After further enlargements from 1953 to 1967 and present installations for the handling of containers Haydarpaşa is the largest port area of Istanbul (LEITNER 1967, after p. 97).

A little to the north is Harem, the landing stage for the commercial ferry (lorries, busses) from Sirkeci until the opening of the first bridge across the Bosphorus in 1973. Large vehicles are still being ferried. Very long, broad and high, optically prominent breakwaters protect the quays from the often strong southwesterly winds (Turkish: lodos).

Of the other large buildings the most spectacular is the gigantic, rectangular Selimiye barracks (Turkisch: Selimiye Kışlası), 200 x 267 meters, with its four large towers at the corners, seven storeys high – to be seen from the Bosphorus from afar, a landmark (SUMNER-BOYD & FREELY 1972, p. 429; YERASIMOS 2000, p. 359).

It stands on a historically important site: there was once – at Sultan Süleyman's the Magnificent time – the Kavaksarayı, an early Ottoman palace, purposely built opposite the Topkapı Sarayı (KREISER 2001, p. 218) – contributing to the symmetrical arrangement of (earlier) Ottoman palaces along the axis of the Bosphorus (Rumeli Hisarı – Anadolu Hisarı, Rumeli Kavağı – Anadolu Kavağı). The Kavaksarayı was the starting point of Ottoman campaigns in Anatolia and beyond.

A forerunner of the present gargantuan (SUMNER-BOYD & FREELY 1972, p. 429) building was a smaller construction of wood, dating from Sultan Selim III. (1789-1807) time. It was later enlarged and made of stone by Mahmut II. (1808-1839) and Abdülmecit I. (1839-1861) (SUMNER-BOYD & FREELY 1972, p. 429). The building was meant – after the destruction of the Janissaries in 1826 – to accommodate the new troops. It is the place that played an important role during the Crimean War (1853-1856), when Florence Nightingale did her humanitarian work there. The pure baroque Selimiye mosque from 1803-1804 was a contribution by Sultan Selim III. (1789-1807) (GOODWIN 1971, p. 413; SUMNER-BOYD & FREELY 1972, p. 430; YERASIMOS 2000, p. 358).

There are more large buildings with impressive sights in the neighbourhood making good use of the level ground. One of them is the present Marmara University which was once a medical school built in 1903 by a German architect (BAEDEKER 1914, p. 225).

The movement of the shipping traffic being level with the sea and the port facilities being not too conspicuous – except the equipment for handling the containers and the grain silos – the view from the Bosphorus is not obstructed. It is easily possible to perceive the outstanding architectural landmarks at the Anatolian side of the southern entrance to the Bosphorus sea- and landscape from the water.

5.16 The Üsküdar Section

The Ottomans occupied the eastern, Anatolian side of the Bosphorus long before the conquest of Constantinople in 1453 – though Constantinople managed to enlarge its Anatolian bridgehead from time to time (PITCHER 1972, maps VIII-XIII). It was already Beyazıt I. Yıldırım (1389-1402) who – in 1390 – ordered Anadolu Hisarı to be built, the castle corresponding to Rumeli Hisarı on the western side (SUMNER-BOYD & FREELY 1972, p. 505).

After the conquest of Constantiople Üsküdar – being situated opposite the old quarters of the city of Istanbul – became the ferry port for crossing the lower Bosphorus. Soon after the conquest Üsküdar began to accumulate a number of historically and architecturally important mosques.

It is this collection of mosques – five at the water's edge or near to it, and four others in the densely built-up urban area – that made Üsküdar, its shore and skyline, a very important section of the Bosphorus sea- and landscape.

The most prominent of these mosques is the Iskele camii, prominent because it stands next to the landing stage of Üsküdar, on an elevated platform or terrace, has two minarets at the sea front and is comparatively large (GOODWIN 1991, p. 212; SUMNER-BOYD & FREELY 1972, p. 420; MÜLLER-WIENER 1997, p. 424 – with groundplan). The other name of the mosque is Mihrimah Sultan camii – not to be confused with a second Mihrimah Sultan camii near the great Theodosian land wall at the Edirne gate. Mihrimah was the daughter of Sultan Süleyman I. the Magnificent (1520-1566) and wife of the Grand Vezir Rüstem Paşa.

The mosque was built in 1548 by the most famous of Ottoman architects, Sinan. Mihrimah is supposed to have been displeased with the mosque and therefore asked Sinan to build another one for her, the one near the Edirne gate (SUMNER-BOYD & FREELY 1972, p. 421).

The arrangement around the mosque is a külliye: there is a medrese, which is nowadays differently used; a mekteb (English: religious shool for boys), two mausoleums (Turkish pl.: türbelar) and the şadırvan stands in front of the mosque in its main axis under a large roof. The architecture of the mosque is unusual: only three (instead of two or four) semi-domes support the central dome – perhaps because a hill is right behind the mosque.

The large, handsome fountain near the mosque is only locally connected with it. This baroque type of a fountain dates from 1762, Sultan Ahmet III. (1703-1730) time (SUMNER-BOYD & FREELY 1972, p. 421; MÜLLER-WIENER 1977, p. 424 – groundplan).

Not far away is the Yeni Valide camii (GOODWIN 1971, p. 365; SUMNER-BOYD & FREELY 1972, p. 422) – not to be mixed up with another Yeni Valide camii, the one at Eminönü. It dates, like the fountain near the Mihrimah mosque, from Ahmet III. (1703-1730) time, built from 1708 until 1710, in classical style, before the baroque influence began (SUMNER-BOYD & FREELY 1972, p. 427). It is a külliye-type assembly with mekteb or darülhadis (English: school of religious law) – later used as a library – imaret, çeşme, sebil and the türbe of Ahmet III. mother Gülnus Emetullah.

Next comes an extremely pittoresque little mosque, the Şemsi Paşa camii from 1580, another work of Sinan, built for the Vezir Şemsi Paşa (SUMNER-BOYD & FREELY 1972, p. 422; MÜLLER-WIENER 1977, p. 484 – with groundplan). It stands right at the water's edge, separated from the Bosphorus only by a fashionable promenade. The medrese/darülhadis is a rectangular, winged construction forming two sides of the courtyard; a stone wall with grilled windows on the other sides makes the little külliye particularly beautiful. It can only be hoped that the construction of the Bosphorus tunnel railway station, which is presently (2006) going on between the Iskele camii and the Şemsi Paşa camii, will not disturb too munch the sites of these two mosques.

Half way up a low hill – therefore perceptible from the Bosphorus – is the next one of the early mosques at Üsküdar, the Rum Mehmet Paşa camii (SUMNER-BOYD & FREELY 1972, p. 423; MÜLLER-WIENER 1977, p. 456 – with groundplan; cp. GOODWIN 1971, p. 283 – photo). It dates from 1471. Rum Mehmet Paşa was the Grand Vezir of Sultan Mehmet II. Fatih (1451-1481), the conqueror of Constantinople.

Today's architects believe there is a strong Byzantine influence to be seen in the building (SUMNER-BOYD & FREELY 1972, p. 423). A medrese, a hamam, a çeşme and the sinister türbe of Rum Mehmet Paşa were part of the original külliye, but the medrese and the hamam disappeared (MÜLLER-WIENER 1977, p. 417).

A little farther up the slopes is the Ayazma camii from 1760-1761, of Sultan Mustafa III. (1757-1774) time, dedicated to his mother (GOODWIN 1971, p. 387; SUMNER-BOYD & FREELY 1972, p. 423) – evaluated as one of the more successful baroque mosques. The dome and the minaret of the mosque form part of the skyline of this area (GOODWIN 1971, p. 283 – photo).

The other four mosques of rank at Üsküdar are away from the Bosphorus, hidden in the urban housing and commercial sprawl.The most outstanding is the great külliye of the Atik Valide camii, dating from 1583, built by Sinan for Nur Banu Sultan, the wife of Selim II. (1566-1574) and mother of Murat III. (1574-1595) (GOODWIN 1971, p. 289; SUMNER-BOYD & FREELY 1972, pp. 425-427 – with groundplan; MÜLLER-WIENER 1977, pp. 402-403 – with groundplan). The mosque is also called Eski Valide camii (MÜLLER-WIENER 1977, p. 402).

It is the model of an extensive külliye with originally – besides the mosque with the two minarets – a medrese/darülhadis, mekteb, imaret, darülkurra (English: for Koran readers), darüşşifa/şifahane (English: hospital), a double hamam, a şadırvan and even a kervansaray (English: caravansary) (SUMNER-BOYD & FREELY 1972, p. 426 - groundplan; MÜLLER-WIENER 1977, p. 402). Unfortunately part of the külliye-buildings have in modern times been used as a prison or have suffered from extensive damage (MÜLLER-WIENER 1977, p. 403). Only part of the arrangement, the rooms of the hospital, have been restored (GOODWIN 1971, p. 290).

The other two mosques within the urban area of Üsküdar are the Ahmediye and the Çinili mosques (SUMNER-BOYD & FREELY 1947, pp. 424, 428). The Amediye built in 1722 in classic style in Ahmet III. (1703-1730) time, is a külliye, of which a library and a lecture hall (Turkish: dershane) are the most attractive buildings (SUMNER-BOYD & FREELY 1972, p. 424). The Çinili mosque belongs to a small külliye built in 1640 by Sultan Valide Mahpeyker Kösem, the mother of Murat IV. (1623-1640).

Finally still another historical and cultural attraction on the border to the Harem - Haydarpaşa area is part of the Üsküdar section: the Kız Kulesi (MÜLLER-WIENER 1977, p. 334; SUMNER-BOYD & FREELY 1972, p. 431). The edifice itself is not attractive at all – it is its site and situation: it stands on a rock that pierces the sea level, right in the water of the Bosphorus, a few hundred meters away from the Anatolian coast.

The rock belongs to a submarine ridge running from Üsküdar to Sirkeci. This will be the route of the Bosphorus railway tunnel presently and at least until 2009 under construction (STEWIG 2006).

A forerunner of the present tower is supposed to have been built by one of the Byzantine emperors in the 12th century, Manuel Comnenus (1143-1180) as a lighthouse and as the eastern support of a floating chain closing the Bosphorus for shipping (MÜLLER-WIENER 1977, p. 334). Since the beginning of the 19th century the Kız Kulesi acquired several other functions in connection with shipping (as a quarantine-, as a semaphore- and as a customs-station); it was also the home of retired naval officers (SUMNER-BOYD & FREELY 1972, p. 431).

The modern usage is very different: the tower served for the final scene of the James Bond film "The World is not enough" (GORYS 2003, p. 174) and is now a fashionable and costly restaurant to be reached by boat from the side of the Şemsi Paşa mosque and offers romantic evenings on the moonlit Bosphorus.

The great number of architecturally important mosques at Üsküdar, three of them built by Sinan, the most famous of Ottoman architects, five of them facing the Bosphorus or crowning the Üsküdar skyline, furthermore the pittoresque situation of the Kız Kulesi make the Üsküdar section a most graceful addition to the Bosphorus sea- und landscape.

It can only be hoped that the underground Üsküdar railway station beside the Iskele mosque and near the landing stage of the Bosphorus ferries as the entrance to the Bosphorus tunnel will not disturb the pleasant assembly of the mosques at the water's edge.

5.17 The Kuzguncuk-Beylerbeyi- Çengelköy Section

The center-piece of this section is not the first Bosphorus suspension bridge, the Boğaziçi Avrupa Köprüsü opened in 1973, which crosses the Bosphorus from Ortaköy, but it is – after the Dolmabahçe Sarayı and the Çırağan Sarayı – the third 19th century grand palace of the Ottoman ruling family – built at a time when the Ottoman state was already a great debtor – the Beyerlerbeyi Sarayı, which is unfavourably dwarfed by the near and very high pylon of the Bosphorus bridge.

The Beylerbeyi Sarayı was constructed in the reign of Sultan Abdulaziz (1861-1876) in 1865 by Sarkis Balyan (SUMNER-BOYD & FREELY 1972, p. 508) or by both Sarkis and Agop Balyan (GOODWIN 1991, p. 422) of the Balyan clan of architects. Like the Dolmabahçe Sarayı and the Çırağan Sarayı the Beylerbeyi Sarayı had forerunners – when the palace built in the reign of Mahmut II. (1803-1839) from 1826 to 1827 burned down it was replaced by a new one (GÜLERSOY 1973, p. 287). According to YERASIMOS (2000, p. 370) the old palace was built from 1829 to 1832 by Kirkor Balyan and burned down in 1851.

The Beylerbeyi Sarayı (YERASIMOS 2000, p. 272 – groundplan of the first floor) – originally meant to be only a summer residence – is smaller than the Dolmabahçe Sarayı. It stands like its predecessor immediately at the water's edge. The architecture of the palace – completely built of marble – is praised by modern architects because it is well proportioned and comparatively plain in style – compared with the excessive decorations of the Dolmabahçe palace. On each side of the palace, directly at the Bosphorus, stand little pavilions of stone – their roofs in the form of a tent – which were used for the separate arrival and departure of men and women (YERASIMOS 2000, p. 272).

The palace served as a guest home for visitors of the Ottoman ruling family (SUMNER-BOYD & FREELY 1972, p. 508). The interior of the palace (GÜLERSOY 1973, pp. 287-291, 291-297; HELLIER & VENTURI 1994, pp. 194-199) is entirely in European style, an eclectic French Empire style with oriental additions (HELLIER & VENTURI 1994, p. 194).

The Dolmabahçe Sarayı like the Beylerbeyi Sarayı is today a museum (GORYS 2003, p. 211). Originally a large garden belonged to the palace and an extensive deer park, the Cemil Bey Korusu; this was a little disfigured by the high-rise approach motorway to the Bosphorus bridge.

The situation being similar to that of the Dolmabahçe and Çırağan palaces – there was no proper mosque for the performance of the religious rituals in the palaces – a mosque, with two minarets, was used, a little away, in the direction of Çengelköy, near the Beylerbeyi landing jetty, directly at the water's edge, like so many other mosques that grace the shores of the Bosphorus. On some maps this Beylerbeyi mosque is called Hamid-i-Evvel camii. It was erected in 1778 in the reign of Abdülhamit I. (1774-1789) (SUMNER-BOYD & FREELY 1972, p. 508). It is devoid of monumentality and adopted to the surrounding nature (YERASIMOS 2000, p. 352 – photo; cp. GORYS 2003, p. 173 – photo; HINKLE & SLUIS 2003, p. 87 – photo).

The Beylerbeyi palace (together with the Bosporus bridge) is the center of this section at the eastern side of the Bosphorus. It extends southwards to Kuzguncuk and northwards to Çengelköy (SUMNER-BOYD & FREELY 1972, pp. 508, 509).

There are several small mosques on the shore or nearby which may be classed as neighbourhood mosques (Kurızguncuk camii and Cemil Molla camii in the Kuzguncuk part, Hacı Ömer camii and Hambullah Paşa camii in Çengelköy) which was originally a fishingvillage, with a baroque fountain, and a little harbour.

South of the Bosphorus bridge exists the large area of the Deniz Astsubay Lisesi (English: Naval Training College for Non-Commissioned Officers), an architecturally unimportant building.

This is the section where – on the eastern side of the Bosphorus – summer houses/residences (Turkish sing.: yalı) come in in greater numbers: Kuzguncuk has the famous Mocan/Fethi Ahmet Paşa yalı, Çengelköy the not less famous Sadullah Paşa yalı (HELLIER & VENTURI 1994, pp. 79-149); other yalıs are the Madam Agavni Muratyan yalı (Kuzguncuk), the Kamil Paşa yalı, the Halil Haşim Bey yalı, the Izzet Reha Poroy yalı (Beylerbeyi), and the Bostancıbaşı Abdullah Ağa yalı, the Server Bey yalı, the Muazzez Hanım yalı (Çengelköy) (HINKLE & SLUIS 2003, pp. 84-89).

The fashion of having summer houses on the shores of the Bosphorus dates back to early Ottoman times, when wooden palaces were built by the Ottoman aristocray on both sides of the Bosphorus (KREISER 2001, pp. 218-228). This fashion spread in the course of history to the well-to-do and to the not-so-well-to-do nowadays. In Ottoman and later times Levantine and non-Levantine businessmen shared the enjoyment of life in stately residences at the water and in the surrounding gardens in summer time as well as the processions on the Bosphorus to and from the houses. All this was part of what has been called (French) "civilisation du Bosphore" (MANTRAN 1962, p. 85; cp. HELLIER & VENTURI 1994, p. 90).

The two famous yalılar (Turkish plural) in Kuzguncuk and Çengelköy date from the 18th century (HELLIER & VENTURI 1994, pp. 78, 79, 100, 111, 149). The Mocan Fethi Ahmet Paşa/Pink yalı in Kuzguncuk, in pink colour, of modern construction, with slender pillars supporting part of the upper floor, is supposed to have inspired the French architect Le Corbursier, when he stayed in Istanbul in 1911, to his monumental housing blocks on pillars, such as the Unité d'Habitation in Marseille (HELLIER & VENTURI 1994, pp. 78, 79 – photo; HINKLE & SLUIS 2003, p. 91 – photo). The other famous yalı, the Sadullah Paşa yalı, was built in 1783 and is one of the oldest and most beautiful wooden yalıs (HINKLE & SLUIS 2003, p. 86 – photo).

In a way the eastern, Anatolian side of the lower Bosphorus is different from the western, Thracian side. On the western side the tertiary sector with its high development potential has since a long time expanded northwards along the coast (LEITNER 1971, pp. 58-61), where offices for public and business administration and installations for tourism, large international hotels, compete with the splendours of the Bosphorus for land use. This is now the case on the western side even beyond the first Bosphorus bridge.

On the eastern side there is the collection of famous, revered mosques at Üsküdar. Admittedly the tertiary sector plays a leading role at Haydarpaşa and Harem in the form of railway and shipping installations and – away from the coast – in the form of services for the urban population of Kadıköy and Üsküdar. But large international hotels are lacking and there is little expansion northwards along the Bosphorus.

So, north of Üsküdar the land use of the area and its atmosphere changes considerably and is dominated by residential functions. Leisure and quietude, typical of many parts of the Bosphorus sea- and landscape, take over.

5.18 The Kuleli-Vaniköy-Kandilli Section

Parks and gardens are the dominant land use of this section. One of these large parks originally belonged to the Ottoman ruling family (KREISER 2001, p. 260). The natural character of the coastline is a contrast to the character of the opposite side of the Bosphorus: Arnavutköy is urban. Some of the architectural attractions of the Kuleli-Vaniköy-Kandilli section hide in the parks and gardens. This is a section where a great number of yalıs stand on a small coastal strip with relatively steep and wooded slopes behind. Most of them belonged originally to ministers, authors or musicans of the late Ottoman period (HINKLE & SLUIS 2003, pp. 77-82).

From south to north the yalıs of Vaniköy are: Iffet Hanım yalı, Mahmud Nedim Paşa yalı, Anadolu Kazasker Necmettin Efendi yalı, Serasker Rıza Paşa yalı, Ahmet Nazif Paşa yalı, Fazıl Bey yalı, Kadın Efendi yalı, Recaizade yalı; to Kandilli belong the Edip Efendi yalı, Hadi Semi Bey yalı (HINKLE & SLUIS 2003, p. 77). None of them reached the rank of fame. One of them, the oldest, is the yalı of the Grand Vezir Daman Ibrahim Paşa of Ahmet III. (1703-1730) time (HELLIER & VENTURI 1994, p. 16).

There are also some mosques at or near the water, the Kandilli camii, the Vaniköy camii and – very attractive – the wooden little Kaymak Mustafa Paşa camii in pink colour with a rather short minaret (HELLIER & VENTURI 1994, p. 15 – photo without caption), directly beside the Bosphorus (HINKLE & SLUIS 2003, p. 83 – photo).

There is a large, architecturally moderately interesting, historically important, gigantic building, also directly at the Bosphorus, the Naval Officers' Training College (Turkish: Kuleli Askeri Lisesi). It has a tremendous length, immediately at the water, is three storeys high, with a flight of entrance stairs and two high-rise towers, each six storeys high (HELLIER & VENTURI 1994, pp. 12, 13; HINKLE & SLUIS 2003, p. 83 – photo).

It was constructed in 1828 in the reign of Mahmut II. (1808-1859) after the destruction of the elite army corps of Janissaries in 1826 who had become a state within the state, to house the new troops (KREISER 2001, p. 259). The present sea front of the building dates back to the time of Abdülaziz (1861-1826). In 1859 the then barracks was the site an unsuccessful conspiracy of officers and religious leaders against Abdülhamit I. (1839-1861) (KREISER 2001, pp. 260-261). The conspirators were sentenced to death but remained imprisoned.

The buildings of two other institutions are hidden in the parks of the area. One has a tradition reaching back to the 19th century. It is the palace – built in 1850 on high a hill – of Adile Sultan, the sister of Sultan Abdülaziz (1861-1876). It is now used as a Junior College for Girls (Turkish: Kandilli Kız Lisesı) (SUMNER-BOYD & FREELY 1972, p. 507; HINKLE & SLUIS 2003, p. 79). From it one has a grand view of the Bosphorus. The other institution – away from the Bosphorus – is a scientific one, an observatory, meteorological station and earthquake research institute (Turkisch: Kandilli Rasathanesi ve Deprem Araştırma Enstitüsü).

On the whole – with some exceptions – the green colour dominates the sea front of this section from Vaniköy to Kandilli – not untypical of many parts of the Bosphorus sea- and landscape.

5.19 The Anadolu Hisarı Section

This is another jewel of the Bosphorus sea- and landscape: a medieval castle, a neat little 19th century palace, two stately 18th century summer residences and several other yalıs and an ancient open air mosque (Turkish: namazgah) – all set in a scenic natural arrangement on the side of the Bosphorus.

The Anadolu Hisarı corresponds to the Rumeli Hisarı on the other side. Together the two castles were able to completely close the Bosphorus. Their topographical situations are quite different. The Rumeli Hisarı sits on the lower slope of a hill across a little valley. Anadolu Hisarı – not so well restored as Rumeli Hisarı, – stands on a spur of low land between the little Göksu river and the Bosphorus (MÜLLER-WIENER 1977, pp. 332-333 – groundplan).

The inner part of the Andolu Hisarı was a keep (SUMNER-BOYD & FREELY 1972, p. 505) built much earlier than Rumeli Hisarı, about 1390 in the reign of Beyazıt I. (1389-1402), when the Ottoman advance from Anatolia reached the Bosphorus (MÜLLER-WIENER 1977, p. 332). The outer wall, together with a barbican, was probably added at the time of Mehmet II. (1451-1481) when he had Rumeli Hisarı constructed in preparation for the siege of Constantinople, i. e. shortly before 1453. Of the originally existent several tall towers one is left over. Like Rumeli Hisarı Anadolu Hissarı experienced a time of decay when the old function of the two castles became redundant. There were some restaurations in 1928/29 (MÜLLER-WIENER 1977, p. 333).

The ancient open air mosque (Turkish: namazgah) (MÜLLER-WIENER 1977, p. 333 – groundplan) is nearby. It is made of stone, the prayer niche (Turkish: mihrab) – in the direction of Mecca – and the pulpit (Turkish: mimber). It was built between 1660 and 1780 (SUMNER-BOYD & FREELY 1972, p. 506).

An extreme contrast – architecturally, historically and functionally – is the Küçüksu Kasrı, the neat palace beside the other little river, the Küçüksu. It was styled in 1856 bei Nikoğos Balyan of the Balyan clan of Ottoman architects in the reign of Abdülmecit I. (1839-1861) (YERASIMOS 2000, p. 368; SUMNER-BOYD & FREELY 1972, p. 506). It has – on the outside – a straight entrance stairway from the garden and an impressive horseshoe-like stairway on the Bosphorus side; it abounds – not unusual for the time and the architect – with abundant decorations (YERASIMOS 2000, p. 368; HELLIER & VENTURI 1994, pp. 178, 182-185).

The two stately summer residences are the Kıbrıslı Mustafa Emin Paşa yalı and the Count Ostrorog yalı (SUMNER-BOYD & FREELY 1972, pp. 506-507). The Kıbrıslı yalı – named after the original owner who came from Cyprus (Turkish: Kıbrıs) and was Grand Vezir for Sultan Mehmet I. (1730-1754) (HELLIER & VENTURI 1994, p. 85) – covers a stretch of 64 meters at the Bosphorus quay, was built of wood in about 1760 (SUMNER-BOYD & FREELY 1972, p. 506). It is a one storey residence, only the central part has two storeys. The sea front had been given a light blue colour (HELLIER & VENTURI 1997, pp. 85/86; HINKLE & SLUIS 2003, p. 78 – photo). The ground plan has a cross-like arrangement with four corner rooms (HELLIER & VENTURI 1994, p. 89). This lay-out is traditional with the older summer residences and goes back to pre-Ottoman Turkish and Central Asian patterns of tents and houses (HELLIER & VENTURI 1994, p. 89).

The other stately summer residence is that of the original owner Count Ostrorog, who was judicial adviser to Ottoman rulers. It was built about 1790 (SUMNER-BOYD & FREELY 1972, p. 507). It is a two storey wooden construction in dark red-brown colour and has one of these garages below the main floor into which boats can be directly pulled from the Bosphorus as in many other summer residences at the water (HELLIER & VENTURI 1994, pp. 80-81; HINKLE & SLUIS 2003, p. 78 – photo). There are more yalıs, the Rıza Bey yalı, the Bahriyeli Sedat Bey yalı, the Zarif Mustafa Paşa yalı north of Anadolu Hisarı (HINKLE & SLUIS 2003, p. 73).

The old castle is hidden from view from the side of the Bosphorus by a series of yalıs, which are – from south to north – the İnönü yalı, the Şeyh Talat Efendi yalı, the Manastırlı Ismail Hakkı Bey yalı and the Köseleçiler yalı (HINKLE & SLUIS 2003, p. 73). Just south of the Fatih Sultan Mehmet Bosphorus bridge is another series of yalıs (HINK-LE & SLUIS 2003, p. 66): the Hekimbaşı yalı, the Marki Necip yalı, the Nuri Paşa yalı and the perhaps most famous of all the old yalıs, the Amcazade Hüseyin Paşa yalı, also called Köprülü yalı –unfortunately in a dilapidated state (HELLIER & VENTURI 1994, p. 23 – photo; HINKLE & SLUIS 2003, p. 72 – photo).

It is the oldest yalı in wood, from 1698, but the Haremlik is gone, only the Selamlık protruding over the water (GÜLERSOY 1973, pp. 301-305; HELLIER & VENTURI 1994, pp. 22, 23, 100-111). The owner of the yalı at the time of construction was a member of the fifth generation of the Köprülü dynasty of high ranking officials serving the Ottoman ruling family as grand vezirs and admirals; some were killed after unsuccessful battles (HELLIER & VENTURI 1994, p. 106).

The Selamlık protruding over the water has windows on three sides allowing grand views of the Bosphorus. The original decorations inside were painted flower decorations with Arabic and Persian influence – typical of the fashionable artistic style of the Tulip Period (1718-1730) (Turkish: Lale Devri) of Ottoman culture (HELLIER & VENTURI 1994, p. 106).

In the Köprülü yalı the Treaty of Karlowitz between the Ottoman state and Austria was ratified in 1699. It meant the beginning of territorial reduction from empire size for the Ottoman state. The Treaty of Küçük Kaynarca was also signed in the Köprülü yalı, in

1734, which brought the loss of the Crimean area for the Ottoman Empire and the opening of the Straits for Russia (HELLIER & VENTURI 1994, p. 111).

The assembly of buildings and homes from Anadolu Hisarı to the Ostrorog yalı is set on level ground, a meadow between the two little Küçüksu and Göksu rivers. At the upper Golden Horn two little rivers, the Alibeyköy and the Kağıthane, empty their water into the Haliç. They have – in the past – been given – by Europeans – the name Sweet Waters of Europe. As a counter-piece the two little Küçüksu and Göksu rivers are called the Sweet Waters of Asia (SUMNER-BOYD & FREELY 1972, p. 506).

The meadow between the two rivers with its lovely setting and stately surroundings was a resort in Ottoman times where the fashionable world met. Mihrişah Sultan, the mother of Sultan Selim III. (1789-1807), had a fountain built for the enjoyment of the early tourists (GOODWIN 1991, p. 410).

The tradition of the place as a resort still holds good, with modern additions: an artificial beach has been filled up and the Göksu river may be used by rowing boats (SUMNER-BOYD& FREELY 1972, p. 506).

All this makes the Anadolu Hisarı section the more precious for the Bosphorus sea- and landscape.

5.20 The Kanlıca Section

A number of similarities exist in the Kanlıca section and the Kandilli section. The south-north coastline turns – in an almost rectangular way – into the west-east direction. So parts of the two sections are exposed to the north, i. e. to the comparatively cold northerly winds from the Black Sea in the hot summer months. This is perhaps the reason for the relatively many summer residences in both sections. Also, in the Kanlıca section the amount of large parks, open green spaces, can well be compared with that in the Kandilli section. And there are no excessively large buildings at the water – except that of the Kuleli Lisesi – in the Kandilli and Kanlıca sections.

Again there is a great number of yalıs, with a wide range of architectural styles, some of most modern constructions. Again relatively steep slopes limit the distribution of the yalıs to an alignment at the water. The yalıs are from south to north (HINKLE & SLUIS 2003, pp. 63, 66): Princess Rukiye yalı, Avukat Emcet Ağıt Bey yalı, Yağlıkçı Hacı Raşit Bey yalı, Sadrazam Kadri Paşa yalı, Ethem Pertev yalı, Hacı Ahmet Bey yalı, Mehmet Muhtar Bey yalı, Yağcı Şefik Bey yalı, 7-8 Hasan Paşa yalı (Asaf Paşa yalı), Ahmet Rasim Paşa yalı, Halil Ethem Paşa yalı. The construction material ranges from wood to glass, steel and concrete; the colour of the houses varies from red brown via pale colours to yellow and white (photos: HINKLE & SLUIS 2003, pp. 67-71) – but all have direct admission to the sea. The best known are the 7-8 Hasan Paşa yalı (Asaf Paşa yalı), resembling a Venetian palace (GOODWIN 1991, p. 441), the Ahmet Rasim Paşa yalı and the Ethem Pertev yalı (HELLIER & VENTURI 1994, p. 136).

The oldest building in the Kanlıca section, however is a little mosque at the village square by Vezir Iskender Paşa. It dates from 1559-1560 and is considered to be a minor work of Sinan (SUMNER-BOYD & FREELY 1972, p. 503). It is dwarfed by the newly installed technological tower for radar surveillance of Bosphorus shipping.

But there is also a most impressive building, a palace in a large park, the Hidiv Kasrı, the former residence of Abbas Hilmi, the last Khedive (viceroy of Egypt), from 1900 (SUMNER-BOYD & FREELY 1972, p. 503; HELLIER & VENTURI 1994, pp. 134, 141; STEWIG 1986, p. 66; HINKLE & SLUIS 2003, p. 65).

The palace has an imposing tower, much higher than the trees of the surrounding park and there are umbrella-like roofs protruding from the tower. Coloured glass has been used for the windows, typical of the decorative style (German: Jugendstil) around 1900 (HELLIER & VENTURI 1994, p. 141). After the departure of the last viceroy of Egypt the palace was not in use for several decades. It was the late Çelik Gülersoy, the Director-General of the Turkish Automobile Club (Turkish: Türkiye Turing ve Otomobil Kurumu) who started the splendid restoration work (HELLIER & VENTURI 1994, p. 141; STEWIG 1986, p. 66).

Grand views of the Bosphorus can be enjoyed from the tower of the palace in almost all directions. But it has to be admitted that in the direction of neighbouring Çubuklu an oiltank farm does not quite fit in with the otherwise half natural – half cultural beauty of the Bosphorus sea- and landscape.

5.21 The Bay of Beykoz Section (Çubuklu - Paşabahçe - Beykoz – Hünkar)

This is a very wide section. The similarities of the area allow to sum up. It has to be stated that part of the area is not an asset to the Bosphorus sea- and landscape, rather a liability. But there are some scenic spots and historical reminiscences. Paşabahçe and Beykoz are old fishing villages (LEITNER 1971, p. 62). In the wide and partly shallow bay of Beykoz some stationary contraptions (Turkish sing.: dalyan) for catching swordfish may still be discovered (SUMNER-BOYD & FREELY 1972, p. 501). At Paşabahçe village is a mosque, built in 1763 by Mustafa III. (1757-1774), the Sultan Mustafa mosque (SUMNER-BOYD & FREELY 1972, p. 502). In the surroundings Beyazıt II. (1489-1522) established large gardens and parks from which the village takes its name (Paşabahçe: English the paşa's garden) (SUMNER-BOYD & FREELY 1972, p. 502) and there was once a little palace built by Hezarpare Ahmet Paşa who was Grand Vezir under Murat IV. (1623-1640).

A few miles away from the Bosphorus and the Hünkar Iskelesi, at Tokat, Fatih Mehmet II. (1451-1481) had a palace and garden built after the conquest of the city of Tokat in northeast–central Anatolia and also a pavilion (Turkish: köşk) at the Hünkar landing pier where he disembarked for his palace (TUCHELT 1962, p. 171). Both decayed. Sultan Süleyman I. the Magnificent (1520-1566) rebuilt the pavilion which again decayed, but was renewed by Mahmut I. (1730-1754) in 1746 (TUCHELT 1962, p. 171). Again the little palace/pavilion was restructured by Sarkis Balyan, one of the Balyan family of architects, about 1850 (SUMNER-BOYD & FREELY 1972, p. 501; HINKLE & SLUIS 2003, p. 61).

At Beykoz a fountain, quite unlike any other Bosphorus fountain, dating from 1746, graces the place (SUMNER-BOYD & FREELY 1972, p. 502). And there is a limited number of yalıs in the Beykoz area, the Niyazi Kaptan yalı, the Hamlıcabaşı yalı and the Ahmet Mithat Efendi yalı (HINKLE & SLUIS 2003, p. 58).

In 1833 a treaty between Russia and the Sublime Porte about shipping privileges and closure of the Straits was signed at Hünkar (MEYER 1908, p. 309). In the wide bay of Beykoz the joint British and French fleets rallied on their way to the Crimea in 1854 at the beginning of the Crimean War (1853-1856) (MEYER 1908, p. 309).

Unlike any other section of the Bosphorus sea- and landscape the Beykoz section has become – quite early – an industrial site (TÜMERTEKIN 1971, 1974-1976, p. 6; STANDL 1994).

In connection with the endeavours of the Ottoman state to reduce dependency from foreign countries for the supply of its army and to adopt modern European development, industrial firms were established at Beykoz and Paşabahçe quite early, towards the end of the 19th century (STANDL 1994, p. 11).

Beykoz acquired a leather and shoe factory (Turkish: Deri ve Ayakkabı Fabrikası) Paşabahçe, in 1884, a glass and bottle factory (Turkish: Şişe ve Cam Fabrikası) (LEITNER 1971, p. 62). They were later joined by a factory producing alcohol, the Yeni Rakı plant (HINKLE & SLUIS 2003, p.63) (Turkish: Ispirto ve Içki Fabrikası). Near Çubuklu is a tank farm (Turkish: Belediye Akaryakıt Deposu) at the water's edge.

During the earlier period of both, migration to cities and industrialization many migrants settled in shanty towns (Turkish pl.: gecekondu evler) near their work places (LEITNER 1971, p. 62; TÜMERTEKIN 1971 p. 21 – map). This happened in the surroundings of Beykoz and Paşabahçe and this spoiled a little the otherwise rural atmosphere.

However the most modern present development is all in favour of beautifying the Bosphorus sea- and landscape in the Beykoz-Paşabahçe area: the leather and shoe factory and the alcohol factory closed down – though the buildings are presently (2006) still there. The glass and bottle factory continues production mainly of artistic glassware – well known, not only in Turkey. It has been given a new administrative building.

The time when the presently still industrial looking area of the Bosphorus sea- and landscape will end – following up the changes at Kuruşeşme and Istinye, on the western side of the Bosphorus, where the beautifying process has been completed – is not far away. Besides, the bay of Beykoz is wide and the coastline of Beykoz and Paşabahçe is a distance away from the mainstream of the Bosphorus where the transit shipping passes.

So even the present sight of the Beykoz section is not too detrimental to the beauty of the Bosphorus sea- and landscape.

5.22 The Anadolu Kavağı Section

From Hünkar to Anadolu Kavağı the coastline resembles in a way the almost purely natural coastline north of Anadolu Kavağı, with a few interruptions like the Turkish Navy salvage yard and the Mobil tankfarm (HINKLE & SLUIS 2003, p. 58).

On the eastern side of the Bosphorus the last stop of the ferries on their northern route is Anadolu Kavağı. The fishing village has become a little resort – at least part of the day: it profits from the lunch-time stop-over of the daily Bosphorus excursion ferries. There is a little harbour for pleasure boats and there are some summer and all-year-round-houses for the not-so-well-to do at the water's edge; the houses have little garages for boats.

Anadolu Kavağı takes its historical importance from its strategic position as sentinel of the northern entrance to the Bosphorus. Above the village and the cliffs, up on the peneplain, are the extensive ruins of a castle facing the Bosphorus – a grand view from the ferries. The origin of this ancient fortification goes back to Byzantine times. The castle (Turkish name: Yoros), which is believed to have been twice as large as Rumeli Hisarı (SUMNER-BOYD & FREELY 1972, p. 499), was later taken over by the Genoese and still later by the Ottomans. Sultan Murat IV. (1623-1640) is supposed to have built – in 1628 – a wall reaching down to the shore and to have fastened a chain across the sea lane to close the Bosphorus against invasions from the north (MEYER 1908, p. 307).

The strategic function continued with the deployment of different technical means. With the help of French military engineers naval batteries were installed below the castle in 1783 by Baron Le Tott and Toussaint and in 1794 by Mounier (SUMNER-BOYD & FREELY 1972, p. 500; HINKLE & SLUIS 2003, p. 57; cp. von MOLTKE 1839, map of the Bosphorus). Even today the Turkish navy is present next to the Anadolu Kavağı village, and there is a kind of yalı, the Marco Paşa villa, on its premises (HINKLE & SLUIS 2003, pp. 58, 59).

After Rumeli Hisarı and Anadolu Hisarı the pair of Rumeli Kavağı and Anadolu Kavağı is once more an example of parallel siting and naming. This clearly is an indication not only of the symmetrical arrangement of castles and villages, palaces and summer residences, harbours and resorts, but it also underlines the fact that – of course – the Bosphorus is the reference axis of the Bosphorus sea- and landscape.

6 The Process of Settlement and Suburbanization in the Bosphorus Sea- and Landscape

Natural and cultural, maritime and terrestrial features – in combination – are the constituent elements of the Bosphorus sea- and landscape. The maritime features are limited to the water area of the Bosphorus, the terrestrial features to the slopes of the surrounding country facing the water area. This is the delimitation of the Bosphorus sea- and landscape.

The analysis may be carried further. The natural features are composed of a number of physical peculiarities. Of these the geological, geomorphological, seismological and climatological characteristics can be found on both, the maritime and terrestrial elements, they are present in the whole of the Istanbul region, the hydrographical character-istics only in the maritime element, in the water area of the Bosphorus – if the short rivers emtying in the Bosphorus are left out of consideration.

The cultural features are composed of a multitude of phenomena, mostly evident on the terrestrial surroundings, on the slopes facing the Bosphorus, but also in the form of shipping and fishing traffic of various kind on the maritime element, the water of the Bosphorus. The man-made cultural features may be divided into the large group of those which are visually perceptible – mosques and palaces, castles and pavilions, houses and residences, parks and gardens, schools and universities, ports and bridges – and the not less large group of those which are not directly perceptible – causes and impacts, motivations and intensions, conflicts and events, explanations and interpretations – the invisible behind the scenes.

There is – of course – another constituent element of the Bosphorus sea- and landscape: its history. Even the physical features of the maritime and terrestrial areas have their own history, that of the formation of the Bosphorus – though this historical dimension differs considerably from that of the man-made cultural features, the history of which is of primary interest in connection with the Bosphorus sea- and landscape.

It is true, historical aspects have been dealt with when the many sections of the cultural features of the Bosphorus sea- and landscape were described and also when some of the events behind the scenes were narrated. So far the historical aspects considered comprised mainly the Ottoman period, in several cases even the early Ottoman period of the Bosphorus sea- and landscape, i.e. roughly 500 years of history. To avoid misunderstandings, the following text is not meant to be a history of the roughly 2000 years of history before the Ottoman period, since the foundation of Calchedon in 680 B.C. and Byzantion in 660 B.C. (MERLE 1916, p. 86). A comparative account of the Bosphorus sea- and landscape before the Ottoman period will, however, shed an interesting and explanative light on the structures which appeared since.

6.1 The ancient Greek period

The first historically recorded settlements were founded in the Bosphorus region in the 7th century B.C. on both sides of the southern entrance to the Bosphorus, on the Anatolian side at Calchedon – a little earlier than on the Thracian side Byzantion. The two settlements belonged to the second wave of ancient Greek colonial expansion which was directed into the Black Sea (STEWIG 1964, fig. 2). The main aim was the establishment of agrarian colonies. For that purpose favourable small areas on the coastline of the Bosphorus and the Black Sea were selected, promontories for an acropolis and a temple and flat, fertile, nearby valley floors for cultivation. At Byzantion the place of the ancient Greek acropolis is today marked by the Topkapı Sarayı, at Calchedon no trace of the early acropolis is left (MÜLLER-WIENER 1977, p. 16).

On the banks of the Bosphorus several relatively separate and independent small Greek colonial settlements, poleis, existed and it is believed (OBERHUMMER 1899, columns 746-755; LEITNER 1971, p. 60) that many promontories of the Bosphorus were once crowned with Greek temples and sanctuaries.

Of the two settlements at the southern entrance to the Bosphorus Byzantion acquired a commercial function as controller of the grain trade – through the Bosphorus as a transit sea lane – from the Greek Black Sea colonies to the Greek homeland cities, especially Athens (MÜLLER-WIENER 1977, p. 16; STEWIG 2006).

6.2 The ancient Roman period

During the last two centuries before and the first two centuries after the birth of Christ the situation of the settlements on the Bosphorus remained unaltered, but the political and the traffic situations changed (STEWIG 2006). With the advance of the Romans in the eastern Mediterranean and the creation of Roman provinces in the northern Balkans and eastern Anatolia two fronts, the Danube front and the Euphrates front, where connected by a military highway east and west of the Bosphorus; the Bosphorus became the crossing station (JIREČEK 1877; STEWIG 1964, fig. 3). The ancient long distance commercial road from Asia did not reach the Bosphorus, but ended – since the Persian advance into Anatolia in the 5th century B. C. – at the Greek harbour cities on the Aegean coast (Miletus, Ephesus); from there maritime traffic continued to the west (STEWIG 1964, fig. 3).

With the coming of the Romans to the Bosphorus Greek political dominance was supplanted by Roman political dominance. In both periods the development of the riverain settlements was determined from outside the region, from Rome or – before – from rivalling Greek cities.

This situation changed fundamentally with the partition of the over-sized Roman Empire into a western region, which decayed because of barbarian invasions in the centuries after Christ, and an eastern region, the east Roman, later Byzantine Empire, which thrived and for which Byzantion became the capital city in 330 A.D. under the name of Constantinople (MÜLLER-WIENER 1977, p. 19). The development of the Bosphorus sea- and landscape was now determined mainly from within the region, from Constantinople.

The cultural situation also changed with the spreading of Christianity in the centuries after Christ. The first churches appeared in the Bosphorus region in the second century (MÜLLER-WIENER 1977, p. 18). When the Christian church amalgamated with the Byzantine state (DUCELLIER et al. 1990) new types of buildings and settlements emerged, characterized by the architecture of cathedrals, churches and monasteries.

6.3 The Middle Age Byzantine period

The first signs of suburbanization appeared with the siting of royal palaces on the Bosphorus by the Byzantine emperors. The extensive publication about Byzantine Constantinople – including the Bosphorus – by JANIN (1964) gives a detailed description of the settlement structure on both sides of the water between roughly 330 and 1453. JANIN listed and located on the western side (JANIN 1964, pp. 465-482) 3 royal palaces, 19 churches, 16 monasteries and 1 asylum for the poor, on the eastern side (JANIN 1964, pp. 482-489) 3 royal palaces, at least 14 churches, 11 monasteries, 4 asylums for the poor and 1 orphanage (cp. MÜLLER-WIENER 1977, p. 22). These institutions seem to have been most numerous on the lower and middle Bosphorus, but monasteries were also founded – a distant away – on the upper Bosphorus.

The political dominance of the Byzantine Empire in the eastern Mediterranean completed the traffic connections of Constantiople and the Bosphorus: from the 7th to the 11th centuries Constantinople became the exclusive world market for exchange between the Orient and the Occident with maritime and terrestrial traffic routes from all directions and across the Bosphorus (STEWIG 1964, fig. 5). The growth of the capital city attracted population. Had the advance of the Romans into the eastern Mediterranean already brought people from their Italian homelands, now merchants from the commercial city republics of Venice, Pisa, Amalfi and Genoa joined them in Constantinople and also Jews, Armeniens and Russians (MÜLLER-WIENER 1977, p. 24). The city of Constantinople and the settlements on the Bosphorus became the homestead of several nationalities and religions among the endogenous Greek population.

During the period of decline and territorial reduction of the Byzantine Empire from the 11th century to 1453 the settlements on the Bosphorus remained as they had evolved before, except for temporary destructions by wars.

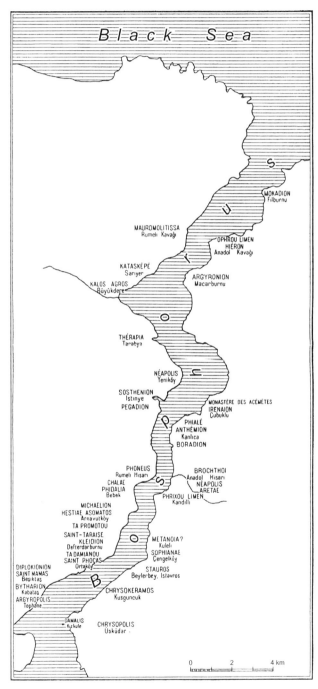

Fig. 3: Byzantine Settlement Locations on the Bosphorus and their Modern Turkish Names
Source: JANIN 1964, map XI

6.4 The early modern Ottoman period

When the Romans pushed into the eastern Mediterranean they came from the west; from the 11th century on the new rulers, Turkish tribes, first the Seljuks, later the Ottomans, came from the east. The Ottomans reached the eastern side of the Bosphorus in the 14th century; Beyazıt I. Yıldırım (1339-1402) had the castle of Anadolu Hisarı built about 1390 (SUMNER-BOYD & FREELY 1972, p. 505).

With the conquest of Constantinople in 1453 Byzantion's political dominance over the Bosphorus and its settlements was supplanted by Ottoman political dominance. Formally the impact exerted on the Bosphorus sea- and landscape by the Ottomans resembled in a way the influence practised in the beginning of the Byzantine area. But of course there were innovations.

The political decisions were again made in the city – now called Istanbul – on the western side of the southern entrance to the Bosphorus. Like the Byzantine Emperors the Ottoman sultans planted palaces and pavilions, gardens and parks on both sides of the Bosphorus at an early stage (TUCHELT 1962).

Again the city became the capital of an empire, the Ottoman Empire, covering territories in Europe, Asia and North Africa; in a way the territorial expansion was similar to that of the Byzantine Empire (PITCHER 1972, map. XVII.).

Once more the growth to empire size attracted maritime and terrestrial traffic from all directions to Istanbul and the Bosphorus (MANTRAN 1962, map. 2). Üsküdar was in the second half of the 17th century the bridgehead of Istanbul on the eastern side of the Bosphorus and with its many caravanseries the terminal (or starting point) of long distance caravan routes from and to many parts of Asia (MANTRAN 1962, pp. 81-83, map 7). And, the old rural and urban settlements on both sides of the Bosphorus continued to exist (MANTRAN 1962, map 2).

But there were, of course, fundamental innovative changes. A new population, the Ottoman Turks, settled in Istanbul and the Bosphorus sea- and landscape as the ruling class. However, parts of the old population, Greeks, Armenians, Jews and others remained. MANTRAN (1962) in his extensive study of Istanbul and the Bosphorus in the second half of the 17th century – at the political zenith and greatest extension of the Ottoman Empire – attempted a roughly quantitative determination of the distribution of Turks, Greeks, Armenians and Jews in the settlements of the Bosporus (MANTRAN 1962, map 8).

From the various countries conquered by the Ottomans in Europe, Asia and Africa people moved to Istanbul and the Bosphorus and this migration continued during the territorial reduction of the Ottoman Empire when refugees came. The result was a motley, a cosmopolitan quality of the population composition in the Istanbul region.

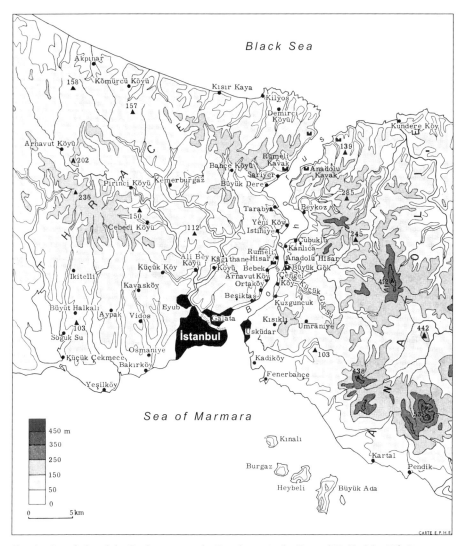

Fig. 4: Istanbul and the Settlements on the Bosphorus in the Second Half of the 17th Century
Source: MANTRAN 1962, map 2

And the cultural situation changed fundamentally. The new population brought with them a new religion. The previously dominant Christian faith was supplanted by the new dominance of the belief in Allah. This meant a new religious architecture was introduced in the Bosphorus sea- and landscape: mosques (Turkish pl.: camilar) and additional edifices like medreseler (English: religious schools), imaretler (English: kitchens for the poor), türbeler (English: mausoleums), şadırvanlar (English: fountains for ritual cleaning), hamamlar (English: bath houses), hanlar (English: caravanseries), darüşşifalar (English: hospitals) and so forth; composite building assemblies (Turkish pl.: külliyeler) spread in the Bos-

The Process of Settlement and Suburbanization

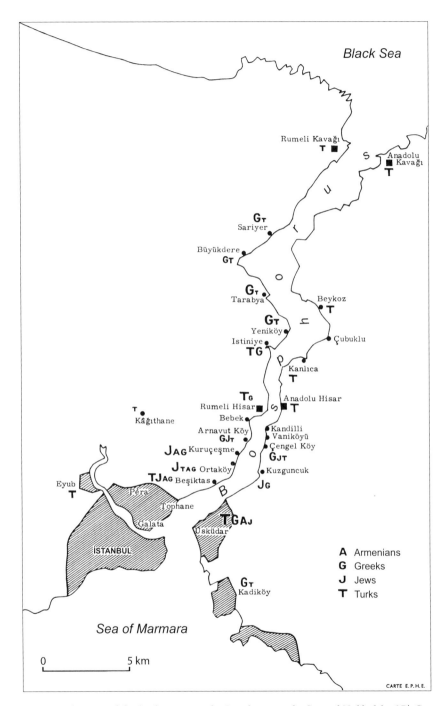

Fig. 5: Population and the Settlements on the Bosphorus in the Second Half of the 17th Century
Source: MANTRAN 1962, map 8

phorus sea- and landscape. A number of the cathedrals and churches was transformed into mosques, but many institutions for the non-Muslim population, churches and synagogues, remained in the Bosphorus settlements for the Christian–Greek and Armenian– and Jewish population. Each group had its own separate cemetery (for example: MANTRAN 1962, map 7). Most of the new mosques were neighbourhood mosques within the urban built–up area of Istanbul, but an Ottoman liking of sites at the water's edge directly on the Bosphorus is clearly evident.

It is doubtful if – during the Byzantine period – high ranking government officials had the habit of having summer residences on the Bosphorus (MANTRAN 1962, p. 85). But during the Ottoman period not only the Ottoman ruling family but also the elevated members of their entourage indulged in and competed in choosing summer residences (Turkish sing.: yalı) at the water's edge, directly on the Bosphorus, in comparativly large numbers (MANTRAN 1962, p. 85). Together with the predilections for gardens and parks and the liking of festivities, processions on the water, culminating in the Tulip Period (1718-1730), a veritable genuine Turkish culture of the yalı, a love for the sweetness of life surrounded by nature (French: la douceur de vivre – MANTRAN 1962, p. 86) evolved in the Bosphorus sea- and landscape. MANTRAN did not hesitate in evaluating this as the singular Ottoman civilization of the Bosphorus (MANTRAN 1962, p. 85: civilisation du Bosphore; cp. PAMUK 2005, p.19, who mentions a Turkish source for the term Bosphorus civilization: Abdülhak Şinasi Hisar, 1887-1963).

Since the 17th century the Ottoman Empire declined and lost most of its territories outside Anatolia. This meant a loss of importance for Istanbul and the Bosphorus as a centre of distribution and traffic connections. Istanbul's function as a world market city had already declined caused by the commercial city republics of Venice, Pisa, Amalfi and especially Genoa, which – though resident in Istanbul during the early Ottoman period – established direct contacts between Europe and the Near East, i. e. modern Levant trade, through the Mediterranean, detouring Istanbul. The discovery of the sea way to India round Africa (STEWIG 1964, fig. 8) and finally the opening of the Suez Canal in 1869 (STEWIG 1964, fig. 8) cost Istanbul the last remnants of important commercial mediator between Europe and the Orient.

6.5 The modern Republican period

After the end of the First World War and the downfall of the Ottoman Empire and the shifting of the capital city of Turkey to the inland city of Ankara in 1923 Istanbul and the Bosphorus sea- and landscape suffered from stagnation (STEWIG 2006). But the societal evolution of Turkey since the 1950ties (STEWIG 1998, 1999, 2000, 2004) secured Istanbul an unprecedented uprise (KEYDER & ÖNCÜ 1993) and growth to a mega city with today more than 10 million inhabitants. This of course had effects on the Bosphorus sea-

and landscape. The basis of Istanbul's spectacular development was its socio-economic performance.

The introduction of the multi-party system, i. e. competing political parties, in Turkey in 1950, the following renunciation of etatism and the new economic policy turning from import substitution via export promotion to liberalization and privatization produced an economic boom in the secondary and tertiary sectors.

Though heavy industries, the iron and steel and the textile industries, preferred locations outside Istanbul – where the raw materials of coal and cotton could be optained directly – Istanbul – the biggest consumer agglomeration of the country – acquired a multitude of consumer industrial branches reaching from pharmaceuticals and electrical and electronic mashinery to ready-made clothing. Istanbul grew to become by far the largest industrial city in Turkey.

In the tertiary sector Istanbul regained the position of Turkey's leading urban place for financial transactions, for retail and wholesale trade, for the organisation of imports and exports, for high ranking education with several universities, for best medical care, for outstanding culture (concerts, opera, plays, films, exhibitions, museums), for tourism – and not merely sightseeing tourism but also for festival and congress tourism and top-ranking sporting events.

The opportunities Istanbul has to offer in jobs, education, leisure and income attracted immigrants from all parts of Turkey, many from the Black Sea coast. Istanbul profited most from the push-pull contrast of living conditions between rural and urban areas in the country. The growing population of migrants and endogenous urbanites in Istanbul differentiated socially in the poor urban class of the newly arrived immigrants, the better-off middle class people working – on the basis of education – mainly in the tertiary sector and the rich upper classes, the industrialists and business men.

The effects of the development of Istanbul on the Bosphorus sea- and landscape differed according to the different location necessities and predilections of the branches of the economy and the social classes.

Of course, the tremendous growth of both, the secondary and tertiary sectors in Istanbul and the extraordinary growth of the population demanded a lot of new space in the Istanbul region, which resulted in the full swing of suburbanization and exceptional extension of the built-up areas on both sides, west and east of the Bosphorus and in a great distance from it.

On the whole the Bosphorus sea- and landscape was – luckily – exempted from industrial suburbanization (TÜMERTEKIN 1970-1971). On the coast of the bay of Beykoz some industrial firms, a leather and shoe factory and the Paşabahçe glasswerks, had established themselves in rural surroundings already in the 19th century (STANDL 1994, p. 11). In the bay of Istinye a dockyard and a floating dock existed since the beginning of the 20th century (TÜMERTEKIN 1974-1975, pp. 2, 19-22). There was a time, in the 1960ties, when the Büyükdere area seemed to get industrialized (TÜMERTEKIN 1974-1975, pp. 2, 22-27) because – for communication reasons – industrial firms look for sites at the water.

But the endeavours of beautifying the Bosphorus sea- and landscape led to the closure and removal of the Istinye dockyard and floating dock and to the closure of the Beykoz leather and shoe and the alcohol factories – though not to the removal of their buildings yet (2006).

The thrust of industrialization in the Istanbul region preferred in the 1960ties the suburban location of Levent (LEITNER 1971, pp. 58-62, map on p. 67) – away from the Bosphorus, on the peneplain, and later (STANDL 1994) the highways leading out of Istanbul on the Thracian and Anatolian side, away from the Bosphorus. So the Bosphorus sea- and landscape was – on the whole – saved from ugly industrial premises.

Communication, and traffic are part of the tertiary sector. When a route runs across land and water the vehicles of transportation need be changed. So in the Bosphorus sea- and landscape port facilities are a necessity. In fact the port of Istanbul extends across the southern entrance to the Bosphorus (ETHEM 1929; LEITNER 1965, 1967; Bundesamt für Seeschifffahrt und Hydrographie 2004, pp. 225-226). The western side of the lower Bosphorus is reserved for commuter passengers on the ferries across the sea lane and for long distance travellers in liners and cruise liners. The eastern side of the lower Bosphorus handles cargo and has new installations for dealing with containers. It is only on the western side where the customs store houses of the Salıpazarı quay mar the view from the Bosphorus and cut off the Tophane assembly from their original site immediately at the water's edge.

Another section of the port of Istanbul, the coal quay at Kuruçesme, which for several decades disgraced a conspicuous part of the western Bosphorus, profited from the beautifying development and has been changed into a park and a posh marina.

Of course, the numerous landing jetties which provide admission for the ferry passengers to the settlements on both sides of the Bosphorus are as much part of the Bosphorus sea- and landscape as the fishing-harbours and marinas for pleasure-boats – but all of them offer pittoresque scenes.

The enormous growth of the population and the built-up areas on both sides of the Bosphorus necessitated a voluminous ferry traffic across the sea lane until in 1973 and 1988 the two suspension bridges were opened. The aesthetic style of both bridges, their full span across the water, and their slender lines – the second bridge is a copy of the first – do not impeach the beauty of the Bosphorus sea- and landscape.

Another kind of maritime traffic is the transit shipping on the Bosphorus. If the dangers connected with the transit of oil-tankers is left out of consideration the wide range of large and small types and curious shapes of ships for passenger and cargo transport add to the colourful scene of the Bosphorus sea- and landscape.

The retail and wholesale trade – as part of the tertiary sector – has its traditional location in the old quarters of the city of Istanbul south and north of the Golden Horn, away from the Bosphorus. The expansion of business administration in Istanbul participated in the suburbanization process, with new office towers in the north, at the terminal of the new metro, at 4. Levent and at Maslak, away from the Bosphorus, but with high-rise buildings to be seen from the Bosphorus – without interfering with the grand views.

Installations for tourist traffic – as part of the tertiary sector – the large international hotels moved into the Dolmabahçe, Beşiktaş and Çırağan sections of the Bosphorus. Ortaköy is the next one. But their modern architectural lines are graceful and not detrimental to the beauty of the respective coastlines; they provide an interesting, variable background and contrast. Only three large modern hotels are sited directly at the water, the Tarabya hotel, the new SAS Radison hotel at Ortaköy and the Kempinski hotel – in the disguise of the Çırağan palace.

The excessive number of (fish-)restaurants, coffee-houses, tea-gardens and other provisions for food and drink, mostly set in shaded gardens and parks at the water for excursion and local tourism and the restored historical pavilions in the Yıldız and Emirgan parks on the western slopes of the Bosphorus add to the pittoresque features.

The education business – as part of the tertiary sector – is also amply present at the Bosphorus. Most of the fine buildings for maritime, military and general education of different levels underline the elegant look of the Bosphorus coastline. The number of universities is astonishing (Mimar Sinan University, Bosphorus University, Marmara University). The museums of Dolmabahçe and Beylerbeyi unite the historical and educational aspects. The Robert College and the Bosphorus University combine the ancient and the modern in admirable park settings.

It may be concluded that the tertiary sector, which is amply present at the Bosphorus in many ways, is a fitting contribution to the lively and up-to-date appearance of the Bosphorus sea- and landscape.

The social classes of the population of Istanbul region have their own location predilections. The poor immigrants, who settled in the gecekondu evler, the shanty towns, in the Istanbul region necessarily choose their housing locations near their working places. The industrialization of Istanbul being almost fully connected with the suburbanization process on the peneplain and the Bosphorus sea- and landscape being almost fully exempted from suburban industrialization, there were only small areas near the Bosphorus with gecekondu evler (TÜMERTEKIN 1974-1976, pp. 16-18) which did not really disturb the beauty of the surroundings.

The middle classes of Istanbul being nowadays economically in a position to participate – to a degree–in the search for summer residences on the Bosphorus – after the model of the ancient Ottoman yalı culture – had to cope with the fact that most of the coastline was already occupied by fashionable and expensive residences, by palaces, museums and educational institutions, by recreational and traffic installations. It seems that the middle classes of Istanbul in their desire for (summer)residences evaded to the upper Bosphorus coastline where the plots are cheaper. But it was possible to buy or rent houses with agreeable exteriors at the water's edge and with little garages for the boats.

For the rich industrialists and businessmen of the Istanbul region a summer residence at the Bosphorus is a must. The problem to find appropriate space at the water – the best lots already occupied for a long time – is being solved this way: the ancient, often decayed yalıs are bought wherever possible.

Some of them have been renovated and restored in the old style (HELLIER & VENTURI 1994). In other places new constructions of the most modern type, made of concrete, steel, glass and stone, replaced old summer residences. The coastal surroundings of Kanlıca are a good example of this latest development.

The style of the modern houses is a break with traditional architectural values, but interesting creations have come into existence, which surely add – though in a different way – to the grace of the Bosphorus sea- and landscape.

7 Evaluation

7.1 The UNESCO World Heritage Convention and Operational Guidelines

In 1972 the United Nations Educational, Scientific and Cultural Organization (UNESCO) passed a resolution and agreed upon a Convention Concerning the Protection of the World Cultural and Natural Heritage (UNESCO 1972). The main distinction was between natural and cultural features. In article 1 a definition is given of what is meant by cultural heritage:

- "monuments: architectural works, ... elements or structures of an architectural nature ... combinations of features of outstanding universal value from the point of view of history, art or science
- groups of buildings: groups of separate or connected buildings ... because of their architecture ... or place in the landscape ... of outstanding universal value from the point of view of history, art or science
- sites: works of man or the combined works of nature and man of outstanding universal value from the historical, aesthetic ... or anthropological point of view."

In article 2 a definition is given of what is meant by natural heritage:

- "natural features consisting of physical and biological formations ... of outstanding universal value from the aesthetic or scientific point of view
- geological and physiographical formations ... of outstanding universal value
- natural sites or natural areas of outstanding universal value from the point of view of science, conservation or natural beauty."

In the Operational Guidelines for the Implementation of the World Heritage Convention (UNESCO 1999) in paragraph 27 details are given concerning the term groups of buildings (in the section about cultural heritage). The term refers to "towns which are no longer inhabited, historic towns which are still inhabited and continue to develop and new towns of the twentieth century."

In the Convention of 1972 and in the Operational Guidelines of 1999 it is stated that there can be significant combinations of cultural and natural features (UNESCO 1972, article 2; UNESCO 1999, paragraph 18) and this led to the acceptance of mixed sites as World Heritage items.

It has been justly criticized by FOWLER (2003, p. 18) that there is more than juxta-position or co-existence when cultural and natural features come together: interaction, interplay, special relationships – one may add: there are system relations between cultural and natural features.

As the result of such thoughts the concept of cultural landscapes, derived from German and French geographers and historians and current in the Berkeley School of Human Geography in the USA in the 1920ties (FOWLER 2003, p. 18), was introduced in 1992 and explained in an amendment to the 1999 Operational Guidelines for the Implementation of the World Heritage Convention (UNESCO 1999, paragraphs 35-42).

Three categories of cultural landscapes are distinguished and two sub-categories (UNESCO 1999, paragraph 39; FOWLER 2003, p. 19).

Of these, category 2 and sub-category 2b – this may be anticipated – fit excellently to the Bosphorus sea- and landscape. For that reason category 2 and sub-category 2b are quoted.

A cultural landscape as

- an organically "evolved landscape" ... "results from an initial social, economic, administrative, and/or religious imperative and has developed its present form by association with and in response to its natural environment. Such landscapes reflect that process of evolution in their forms and component features" (paragraph 39, 2).

A cultural landscape as

- "a continuing landscape is one which retains an active social role in contemporary society closely associated with a traditional way of life. It is continuing to evolve while, at the same time, it exhibits significant material evidence of its historic evolution." (paragraph 39, 2b).

In the UNESCO World Heritage Convention of 1972 one term appears again and again as the top criterion for cultural and/or natural features to be included in the World Heritage list: outstanding universal value – in the fields of history, art, science, anthropology, ethnology, aesthetics, natural beauty, conservation (articles 1 and 2).

Outstanding universal value means uniqueness, irreplaceability, singularity of place. It is admitted that every landscape has a validity as a local place, but of course a cultural landscape of World Heritage rank must have merits above something of only local heritage interest (FOWLER 2003, p. 19).

There are two more criteria a cultural landscape must comply with to be accepted in the World Heritage list: authenticity and integrity. Both are mentioned several times in the Guidelines for the Implementation of the UNESCO World Heritage Convention, the notion of authenticity mainly in connection with cultural features, the notion of integrity with natural features. The test of authenticity is required in design, material, workmanship or setting in the case of cultural landscapes (UNESCO 1999, paragraph 24). Other aspects have been added since 1994 (Nara Conference, Document on Authenticity 1994): form, substance, use, function, tradition, techniques, location, spirit, feeling (FOWLER 2003,

p. 20). In short: authenticity is concerned with the truthfulness, genuineness of features. The notion of integrity is – in the operational guidelines – reserved for natural features (UNESCO 1999, paragraph 44). It means "wholeness, completeness, unimpaired or uncorrupted condition, continuation of traditional uses and social fabrics" (FOWLER 2003, p. 20).

In connection with cultural landscapes, which – this has been pointed out and underlined – are not merely additions of cultural and natural features, but systems, phenomena with interactions, vice versa relations between cultural and natural features, the test of integrity should be enlarged to a test of integration, meaning the character of the influence of nature and man as integral parts of an entity, the harmonious or disharmonious ways of reconciliation between natural and cultural features into a complex unity and totality.

7.2 Singularity and the Bosphorus sea- and landscape

The traditional borderline between the continents of Europe and Asia runs through the Black Sea, the Bosphorus, the Sea of Marmara and the Dardanelles. The mega city Istanbul and the Bosphorus sea- and landscape extend on both sides of the Bosphorus, so the region is situated on two continents – a singularity if this borderline is accepted. In fact the socio-economic conditions on one side of the Bosphorus do not differ from those on the other side. So, to avoid positive and negative connotations of the terms European and Asian it complies better with the factual situation to see the city of Istanbul and the Bosphorus sea- and landscape divided between the two regions of Thracia and Anatolia. But for reasons of touristic promotion the two-continent-theory of Istanbul's situation is being continuously propounded.

The Bosphorus is an international sea lane with an amount of shipping that might be compared with the Suez Canal, the Panama Canal and the Kiel Canal, running right through the middle of a mega city – surely a singularity. Here is a quotation from the UNESCO Operational Guidelines for the Implementation of the World Heritage Convention (1999, paragraph 40): "… long linear areas which represent culturally significant transport and communication networks should not be excluded."

The present function of the Bosphorus as an international sea lane has an enormous historical depth: the legendary Argonauts transited the Bosphorus in the ancient Greek period. It has to be admitted that there were times when the Black Sea was an inland lake of the Ottoman Empire – as long as that empire possessed territories in the Crimea and southern Russia. When the Bosphorus was closed to foreign shipping cabotage dominated, but in the late Ottoman period the Bosphorus was opened again to international shipping. In all, with some interruptions, there was – since ancient Greek times – continuous international sea traffic – a singularity (STEWIG 2006).

The coasts of the Bosphorus, the western more than the eastern, are – with the many restaurants, coffee-houses, tea-gardens, promenades and splendidly restored pavilions in the Yıldız and Emirgan parks, open for the public – an inner urban recreation area (STEWIG 1986).

The combination with the function of international sea lane is a singularity. The function of recreation has – though not for the inhabitants of Istanbul, but for the Ottoman ruling family and high ranking officials – a long historical tradition of building summer residences, pavilions and palaces at the Bosphorus.

The historical dimension of settlements in the Bosphorus sea- and landscape is extra-ordinary – a singularity. Since the planting of Greek colonies at Calchedon in 680 B. C. and at Byzantion in 660 B. C. (MERLE 1916, p. 86) on both sides of the southern entrance to the Bosphorus more than 2600 years of continuous (sub-)urbanization have elapsed. It is true, no material remains of the first settlements exist today, but their sites, though differently used, are unchanged. A view from a ship on the sea lane evokes the former existence of Greek acropolises and Greek temples on the promontories of the Bosphorus.

Another historical fact is also singular: the continuous function of the settlement at the western side of the southern entrance to the Bosphorus being a capital city of two empires, Constantinople as the capital city of the East Roman, later Byzantine Empire from 330 to 1453 and Istanbul as the capital city of the Ottoman Empire from 1453 to 1918/1923. The visible remains of the past in the Bosphorus sea- and landscape, the buildings and groups of buildings at the water's edge and on the slopes facing the Bosphorus, do not go back much further than the Ottoman period, roughly 500 years – which is not a short time.

Except the two castles, the Anadolu Hisarı on the eastern side of the Bosphorus dating from the end of the 14th century and the splendidly restored Rumeli Hisarı dating from the 15th century (1452) on the western side, most of the architectural manifestations of rank were created in the 16th and 19th centuries. In the 16th century it was the most famous of Ottoman architects, Sinan (1490/1491 – 1588) who was responsible for a great number of mosques and their additional buildings, which still exist and are being frequented today. Here is a list of the architectural creations of Sinan in the Bosphorus sea- and landscape (selection from SUMNER-BOYD & FREELY 1972, p. 533-536):

- Hayrettin Barbaros, türbe at Beşiktaş (1541/42)
- Mihrimah Sultan, cami, medrese, mekteb, at Üsküdar (1548)
- Sinan Paşa, cami, medrese, at Beşiktaş (1554/55)
- Hacı Mehmet Paşa, türbe, at Üsküdar (1559/60)
- Iskender Paşa, cami, at Kanlıca (1559/60)
- Molla Çelebi, cami, at Fındıklı (1561/62)

- Yahya Efendi, türbe, medrese, at Beşiktaş (about 1570)
- Kılıç Ali Paşa, cami, türbe, medrese, hamam, at Tophane (1580/81)
- Şemsi Paşa, cami, medrese, türbe, at Üsküdar (1580/81)
- Atik Valide/Nur Banu, cami, medrese, imaret, kervansaray, şifhane, darülkurra, at Üsküdar (1585/86).

Though Sinan's architectural master piece is considered to be his Selimiye mosque at Edirne, his creations at the Bosphorus, when the Ottoman Empire was, under Sultan Süleyman I. the Magnificent (1520-1566) in the zenith of its political and territorial power, are the expressions of Ottoman architectural style of the classic period, a blending of Turkish origins and Byzantine influences (GOODWIN 1971; YERASIMOS 2000).

The second important architectural period manifested in a number of prominent buildings, splendid palaces, pavilions, mosques and summer residences in the Bosphorus sea-and landscape, is the 19th century, a time when the Ottoman Empire was already in political, territorial and financial decline. This period is marked by the Balyan family/dynasty of architects:

- Kirkor (1764-1831) and his son
- Garabed (1800-1866) and his sons
- Nikoğos (1826-1858)
- Sarkis (1831-1899)
- Agop (1838-1875) and
- Simon (1864-1894) (SUMNER-BOYD & FREELY 1972, p. 467; HELLIER & VENTURI 1994, pp 154-182; HINKLE & SLUIS 2003, p. 17; TUĞLACE 1992).

They were responsible for the style of such monuments as the Dolmabaçe palace, the (old) Çırağan palace, the Beylerbeyi palace, the Küçüksu Kasrı, the many palaces and pavilions in the Yıldız park and mosques like the Dolmabahçe mosque, the Nusretiye mosque and others (SUMNER-BOYD & FREELY 1972; HELLIER & VENTURI 1994).

The style of these buildings and groups of buildings – with strong European influence – abounds in opulent baroque decorations; the luxury of these monuments contrasts strongly with the decline of the Ottoman Empire in the 19th century – a singularity?

The outstanding universal value of the Bosphorus sea- and landscape has to do with the architectural style of its monuments, but as much with their spatial arrangement. The monumental palaces and representative mosques (at Dolmabahçe, Çırağan, Beylerbeyi, Üsküdar, Ortaköy) together with other monumental buildings like the Selimiye barracks or the Kuleli Military Training College and the mass of summer residences – according to their number themselves monumental – all have their sites at the water's edge, either directly at the Bosphorus or a little up the slopes facing the Bosphorus. The combination of historical cultural institutions with the water area of the Bosphorus creates beautiful appearances along the coastline.

There exist still more singularities of the Bosphorus sea- and landscape, and they have to do with the historical and present process of suburbanization. The main urban agglomeration being located on the southern entrance to the Bosphorus the suburbanization started from there. It was the ruling Ottoman family that created summer residences on the lower, the middle, later also on the upper Bosphorus – since the 17^h century. Of the earliest residences – mostly small and large wooden pavilions – none survived (TUCHELT 1962). In the course of time they where replaced by opulent ones, built of stone and surrounded by large gardens and parks which added another pittoresque and beautiful element to the Bosphorus sea- and landscape.

The royal Ottoman residences, which had forerunners in the palaces of the Byzantine emperors (JANIN 1964, pp. 468-489), where joined by the summer residences of high- and low-ranking Ottoman officials, who also built their yalıs on the Bosphorus. A historical yalı culture evolved from the 17^h century based on the combination of stately houses, large parks and nearness to the water– a combination of natural and cultural elements.

Together with the festivities and processions to and fro a genuine Ottoman way of life, "la douceur de vivre", was created and has been called "civilisation du Bosphore" (JANIN 1964, p. 85) – a singularity and an outstanding universal value.

The present societal situation of the Bosphorus sea- and landscape is marked by the continuation of the historical yalı culture. It is no longer the ruling Ottoman family that dominates socially, but it is the well-to-do classes, sometimes joined by the not-so-well-to-do, that carry on the old tradition of stately summer residences – some of them restored ancient yalıs, others architecturally extremely modern houses (HELLIER & VENTURI 1994, pp. 79-150; HINKLE & SLUIS 2003).

This situation of the Bosporus sea- and landscape fully complies with paragraph 39 (of the Operational Guidelines for the Implementation of the World Heritage Convention) because it "retains on active social role in contemporary society closely associated with the traditional way of life, and in which the evolutionary process is still in progress. At the same time it exhibits significant material evidence of its evolution over time."

7.3 Authenticity and the Bosphorus sea- and landscape

Authenticity is of course a problem with any cultural landscape of long standing. Manmade and natural catastrophies had and still have deep impacts.

In the Istanbul region it was not only fires that destroyed for instance the Çırağan palace and several of the summer residences on the Bosphorus, but earthquakes too are a great danger. Between 1453 and 1894 49 earthquakes with magnitude at least 5 occurred in the Istanbul region (ERCAN 2001, pp. 53-54). The last very heavy earthquake, magnitude 7, happened in 1894 (EGINITIS 1895) followed by wide-spread destruction. So there can be no guarantee for absolute authenticity of buildings and houses, though of course most of the monuments remained as they were built, some a little neglected or dilapidated.

The old Çırağan palace – burned down in 1910 – has been – after it had remained in ruins for decades – outwardly restored, inside it is a noble hotel of the Kempinski-Group since 1991 (GORYS 2003, p. 189). Excellent restoration and conservation work has been done by Çelik Gülersoy, the late Director-General of the Turkish Automobile Club. Besides the restoration in other areas of Istanbul on the Bosphorus his work was devoted to the many pavilions in the Yıldız and the Emirgan parks, to the Hidiv Kasrı – the former summer palace of the viceroy of Egypt – and to pavilions on the hills of Çamlıca. His restoration work combined historical appearance with modern usage for recreation (STEWIG 1986). The proprietors of a number of yalıs on the Bosphorus invested private money in the restoration of their summer residences (HELLIER & VENTURI 1994, pp. 79-150).

As far as the sites of historical monuments, palaces, pavilions, summer residences, houses, mosques and their additional buildings are concerned they remained at their original places. There are only a few exceptions where – for instance – fountains or bath houses were removed to a different, neighbouring plot when widening of roads urged town-planners to do so.

In a few cases, mostly those of the old külliyeler in the Üsküdar area, some additional buildings like soup kitchens, bath houses, caravanseries or hospitals were either completely demolished or dedicated to new, different functions – in one case that of a supermarket (SUMNER-BOYD & FREELY 1972, p. 421).

7.4 Integrity, integration and the Bosphorus sea- and landscape

The notion of integrity was, in the beginning, reserved as a criterion for natural features to be included in or excluded from the UNESCO World Heritage list (UNESCO 1999, paragraph 44). According to FOWLER (2003, p. 20) – it has been stated – the meaning of integrity is "unimpaired or uncorrupted condition" which brings the notion into the neighbourhord of authenticity. FOWLER (2003, p. 20) suggests as another meaning of integrity:

wholeness, completeness, which is a little different from authenticity. Following this line of thought it is useful to replace the notion of integrity by that of integration.

Integration is a pre-condition of wholeness, completeness, totality. Integration does not merely stand for additions or combinations of things, but means interaction and interrelation. Integration refers to the system character of complex entities. For cultural landscapes being such entities it is advisable to use the notion of integration as a criterion for the decision to include or not include them in the World Heritage list.

The question is: what are its constituent elements, interactions, interrelations, what is its system character? The following natural and cultural features are the constituent elements: the water area of the Bosphorus, the slopes of the coastline facing the Bosphorus, the local and transit ships of the sea lane, the castles, palaces, pavilions, mosques, yalıs, gardens, parks, museums, schools, universities, promenades, restaurants, coffee-houses, tea-gardens and recreational areas, the landing jetties and port installations and, of course, all the people making use of them.

It has to be admitted that there are some other man-made features, which do not quite fit in with the pittoresque and beautiful appearance of the Bosphorus sea- and landscape. These are some port installations, a small number of industrial establishments, a few tank farms and bunker stations. But no doubt, the disagreeable spots of the Bosphorus sea- and landscape are spatially limited and do not impeach the grand and lovely views the extensive natural and cultural features present.

The two new suspension bridges across the Bosphorus, in use since 1973 and 1988 respectively, do not pose an aesthetic problem. With no pillars in the water and their vertical and horizontal lines extremely slender they fit in with the beauty of the Bosphorus sea- and landscape.

There remains a last question: what about the interactions and interrelations of the constituent elements; what about the system character? If the function of the Bosphorus as an international transit sea lane determined by far distant economic powers is left out of account the interactions have local origins. It is the continuous process of settlement and suburbanization which started from the cities at the western side of the southern entrance to the Bosphorus: Byzantion, Constantinople, Istanbul.

The wholeness and completeness of the Bosphorus sea- and landscape, the integration and interrelation of its constituent elements is underlined and convincingly presented by the grid pattern of the most important of its cultural features. The Bosphorus being the central axis these features are symmetrically arranged, from south to north, in Ottoman and Republican times (KR SR 2001, p. 218):

Tokapı Sarayı, the ancient Ottoman central palace, today a museum	—	Selimiye barracks as the place of the original Kavaksarayı, the Ottoman palace opposite the Tokapı Sarayı
Rumeli Hisarı, the well restored Medieval castle	—	Anadolu Hisarı, the partly restored Medieval castle
Rumeli Kavağı, the place of a pre-Ottoman castle (of which no ruins are left), later the site of military installations	—	Anadolu Kavağı, the pittoresque ruins of a pre-Ottoman castle, later the site of military installations
Rumeli Feneri, the lighthouse on the western side of the northern entrance to the Bosphorus	—	Anadolu Feneri, the lighthouse on the eastern side of the northern entrance to the Bosphorus.

These features are the cultural pillars of the network of the Bosphorus sea- and landscape, the knots of the net. The large and imposing rest of cultural features fill the net. The totality presents itself in its interrelations as a system.

7.5 Conclusion

The final conclusion can only be: the Bosphorus sea- and landscape is as a whole and in most of its parts of outstanding universal value. It embodies fully the conditions necessary to be included in the UNESCO World Heritage list, set out in paragraph 39 of the UNESCO Operational Guidelines for the Implementation of the World Heritage Convention, which is herewith repeated: "a continuing landscape … which retains an active social role in contemporary society closely associated with the traditional way of life, and in which the evolutionary process is still in progress. At the same time it exhibits significant evidence of its evolution over time."

8   Publications

ARDEL, A. & A. KURTER (1970-1971): La Topographie Sous-Marine de la Mer de Marmara. In: Review of the Geographical Institute of the University of Istanbul. International Edition. Nr. 13. Istanbul, pp. 1-54.

ATASOY, N. (2004): From Count Ostrorog to Rahmi M. Koç. The Story of a Yalı on the Bosphorus. Istanbul.

AUSTIN, CHR. (1995): Istanbul's Clyde-Built Steam Ferries. In: Ships Monthly 30,12. Burton - on - Trent, pp. 28-30.

BAEDEKER, K. (1914). Konstantinopel, Balkanstaaten, Kleinasien, Archipel, Cypern. Leipzig.

BELGE, M. (2004): Boğaziçi Yalıları, Insanlar. 3rd. edition. Istanbul.

BOIATZIS, I. (1887): Grundlinien des Bosporus. Königsberg. (Dissertation).

BRAUN, F. (1910): Zur Siedlungskunde der Bosporusufer. Beilage zum Programm. Gymnasium Graudenz.

Bundesamt für Seeschifffahrt und Hydrographie (2004): Mittelmeer - Handbuch. Part 5. Levante, Schwarzes Meer und Asowsches Meer. 10th edition. Hamburg, Rostock.

DETHIER, P. A. (1873): Der Bosphor und Constantinopel. Wien.

DUCELLIER, A. & J.-P. ARRIGNON, C. ASDRACHA, M. BALARD, A. CARILE, J. FERLUGA, M. KAPLAN (1986): Byzance et le Monde Orthodoxe. Paris.

DUCELLIER, A. & J.-P. ARRIGNON, C. ASDRACHA, M. BALARD, A. CARILE, J. FERLUGA, M. KAPLAN (1990): Byzanz. Das Reich und die Stadt. Frankfurt, New York, Paris.

EGINITIS, D. (1895): Le Tremblement de Constantinople du 10 Juillet 1894. In: Annales de Géographie. Vol. IV. Paris, pp. 151-165.

ELDEM, S. H. (1993): I. Boğaziçi Yalıları. The Yalıs of the Bosphorus: Rumeli Yakası. European Side. Istanbul.

ELDEM, S.H. (1994): II. Boğaziçi Yalıları. The Yalıs of the Bosphorus: Anadolu Yakası. Anatolian Side. Istanbul.

ERCAN, A. (2001): Marmara' da Deprem. Nerede? Ne Zaman? Ne Büyüklükte? Çare!!! Istanbul.

ERDENEN, O. (1993/1994): Boğaziçi Sahilhaneleri. Istanbul Büyükşehir Belediyesi Kültür Işleri Dairesi Başkanlığı. Vol 1-4. Istanbul.

ERINÇ, S. (1954): The Pleistocene History of the Black Sea and the Adjacent Countries with Special Reference to the Climatic Changes. In: Review of the Geographical Institute of the University of Istanbul. International Edition. Nr. 1. Istanbul, pp. 85-133.

ERINÇ, S. (1986): Géoécologie de la region d'Istanbul. In: Travaux de l'Institut de Géographie de Reims 65/66. Reims, pp. 7-16.

ETHEM, M. (1929): Der Hafen von Stambul und seine Organisation. Borna-Leipzig. (Dissertation).

FOWLER, P. J. (ed.) (2003): World Heritage Cultural Landscapes 1992-2002. UNESCO World Heritage Papers 6. Paris.
FREELY J. & H. SUMNER-BOYD (1986): Istanbul. München.
FREELY, J. (1993): The Bosphorus. Istanbul.
GÖKAŞAN; E. & E. DEMIRBAĞ, F. Y. OKTAY, B. ECEVITOĞLU, M. ŞIMŞEK, H. YÜCE (1997): On the origin of the Bosphorus. In: Marine Geology 140. Amsterdam, Lausanne, New York, Oxford, Shannon, Tokyo, pp. 183-191.
GOODWIN, G. (1971): A History of Ottoman Architecture. Baltimore.
GORYS, A. (2003): Istanbul. Köln.
GÜLERSOY, Ç. (1973): Führer durch Istanbul. Istanbul.
HAMMER, J. von (1822/1967): Constantinopolis und der Bosporus, örtlich und geschichtlich beschrieben. 2 vols. Pesth and Osnabrück.
HELLIER, Ch. & F. VENTURI (1993): Splendours of the Bosphorus. London.
HELLIER, Ch. & F. VENTURI (1994): Villen und Paläste am Bosporus. Meisterwerke der Architektur in Istanbul. München
HINKLE, R. & R. V. SLUIS (2003): From the Bosphorus. A Self-Guided Tour. 2nd edition. Istanbul.
HÖGG, H. (1967): Istanbul. Stadtorganismus und Stadterneuerung. In: BACHTELER, K. (ed.): Istanbul. Ludwigsburg, pp. 281-349. (Karawane – Taschenbuch).
IREZ, F. & H. AKSU (1992): Boğaziçi Sefarethaneleri. Istanbul.
JANIN, R. (1964): Constantinople Byzantine. Paris. (Institut Français d'Etudes Byzantine).
JIREČEK, C. P. (1877): Die Heerstraße von Belgrad nach Constantinopel und die Balkanpässe. Eine historisch-geographische Studie. Prag.
KETIN, J. (1969): Über die nordanatolische Horizontalverschiebung. In: Bulletin of the Mineral Research and Exploration Institute of Turkey. Foreign Edition. Nr. 73. Ankara, pp. 1-28.
KEYDER, Ç. & A. ÖNCÜ (1993): Istanbul and the Concept of World Cities. Istanbul. (Friedrich Ebert Vakfı).
KREISER, K. (2001): Istanbul. Ein historisch-literarischer Stadtführer. München.
KURTER, N. & M. BENER (1962): Introductory Notes on the Geomorphology of Istanbul and its Immediate Surroundings. In: Review of the Geographical Institute of the University of Istanbul. International Edition. Nr. 8. Istanbul, pp. 131-143.
LANGENSIEPEN, B. & A. GÜLERYÜZ (1995): The Ottoman Steam Navy 1828-1923. London.
LEITNER, W. (1965): Die innerurbane Verkehrsstruktur Istanbuls. In: Mitteilungen der Österreichischen Geographischen Gesellschaft. Vol. 107. Wien, pp. 45-70.
LEITNER, W. (1967): Der Hafen von Istanbul. In: BECKEL, L. & H. LECHLEITNER (eds.): Festschrift für L. G. Scheidl. Vol. 2. Wien, pp. 93-107.

LEITNER, W. (1971): Die Bosporus-Landschaft als Beispiel für den Strukturwandel der Istanbuler Außenbezirke. In: Mitteilungen des Naturwissenschaftlichen Vereins Steiermark. Vol. 101. Graz, pp. 55-72.

MAMBOURY, E. (1930): Stambul. Reiseführer. Stambul.

MANTRAN, R. (1962): Istanbul dans la seconde moitié du XVIIe siècle. Essai d'histoire institutionelle,économique et sociale. Paris. (Bibliotheque Archéologique et Historique de l'Institut Français d'Archéologie d'Istanbul, XII.).

MAYER, R. (1943): Byzantion – Konstantinupolis – Istanbul. Eine genetische Stadtgeographie. Akademie der Wissenschaften in Wien. Philosophisch-historische Klasse. Denkschriften. 71. Band, 3. Abhandlung. Wien. Leipzig.

MERZ, A. & L. MÖLLER (1928): Hydrographische Untersuchungen in Bosporus und Dardanellen. Veröffentlichungen des Instituts für Meereskunde. Neue Folge. A. Geographisch-naturwissenschaftliche Reihe 18. Berlin.

MEYERS Reiseführer (1908): Türkei, Rumänien, Serbien, Bulgarien. 7th edition. Leipzig und Wien.

MOLTKE, H. von (1893): Briefe über Zustände und Begebenheiten in der Türkei aus den Jahren 1835 bis 1839. 6th edition. Berlin.

MÜLLER-WIENER, W. (1988): Manufakturen und Fabriken in Istanbul vom 15.-19. Jahrhundert. In: Mitteilungen der Fränkischen Geographischen Gesellschaft, 33/34 Erlangen, pp. 257-320.

MÜLLER-WIENER, W. (1997): Bildlexikon zur Topographie Istanbuls. Byzantion - Konstantinupolis – Istanbul bis zum Beginn des 17. Jahrhundert. Tübingen.

MÜLLER-WIENER, W. (1994): Die Häfen von Byzantion, Konstantinupolis, Istanbul. Tübingen.

NICOLLE, D. & Ch. HOOK (2000): Constantinople 1453. The End of Byzantium. Oxford. (Osprey Series: Campaign).

OBERHUMMER, E. (1899): Bosporus. In: Paulys Real-Encyclopedie der classischen Altertumswissenschaft, III. Stuttgart, columns 741-757.

PAMUK, O. (2005). Bosporus-Erkundungen. In: du. 761, Nr. 10. Zürich, pp. 18-20.

PARSONS, T. & S. TODA, S. ROSS, A. BARKA, J. H. DIETERICH (2000): Heightened Odds of Large Earthquakes near Istanbul. An Interaction-Based Probality. In: Science. Vol. 288, pp. 661-665. (American Association for the Advancement of Science).

PAVONI, N. (1961): Die nordanatolische Horizontalverschiebung. In: Geographische Rundschau. Vol. 51. Stuttgart, pp. 122-139.

PENCK, W. (1918): Die geologischen Grundlagen der Untertunnelung des Bosporus. In: Weltwirtschaft. Zeitschrift für Weltwirtschaft und Weltverkehr. VIII. year. Berlin, pp. 158-160.

PENCK, W. (1919): Die tektonischen Grundzüge Westkleinasiens. Beiträge zur anatolischen Gebirgsgeschichte auf Grund eigener Reisen. Stuttgart.

PENCK, W. (1919): Grundzüge der Geologie des Bosporus. Veröffentlichungen des Instituts für Meereskunde. Neue Folge. A. Geographisch-naturwissenschaftliche Reihe 4. Berlin.

PFANNENSTIEL, M. (1944): Die diluvialen Entwicklungsstadien und die Urgeschichte von Dardanellen, Marmarameer und Bosporus. In: Geologische Rundschau. Vol. 34. Stuttgart, pp. 343-434.

PHILIPPSON, A. (1898): Bosporus und Hellespont. In: Geographische Zeitschrift. Vol. 4. Berlin, pp. 16-26.

PITCHER, D.E. (1972): An Historical Geography of the Ottoman Empire from the earliest times to the end of the sixteenth century. Leiden.

SEGER, M. & F. PALENCSAR (2006): Istanbul. Metropole zwischen den Kontinenten. Berlin, Stuttgart. (Urbanization of the Earth, vol. 10).

SHAW, ST. G. & E.K. SHAW (1977): History of the Ottoman Empire and Modern Turkey. Vol. II. Reform, Revolution and Republic. The Rise of Modern Turkey, 1808-1975. Cambridge.

STANDL, H. (1994): Der Industrieraum Istanbul. Genese der Standortstrukturen und aktuelle Standortprobleme des verarbeitenden Gewerbes in der türkischen Wirtschaftsmetropole. Bamberger Geographische Schriften. Vol. 14. Bamberg.

STANDL, H. (2003): Trinkwasser für die Megacity Istanbul. Probleme und Lösungsstrategien. In: Geographische Rundschau. Vol. 55. Braunschweig, pp. 10-16.

STEWIG, R. (1964): Byzanz – Konstantinopel – Istanbul. Ein Beitrag zum Weltstadtproblem. Schriften des Geographischen Instituts der Universität Kiel. Vol. XXII, 2. Kiel.

STEWIG, R. (1964): Der Grundriß von Stambul. Vom orientalisch-osmanischen zum europäisch-kosmopolitischen Grundriß. In: SANDNER, G. (ed.): Kulturraumprobleme in Ostmitteleuropa und Asien. Festschrift für H. Schlenger. Schriften des Geographischen Instituts der Universität Kiel. Vol. XXIII. Kiel, pp. 195-225.

STEWIG, R. (1964): The Evolution of the Street-Pattern of the City of Istanbul since the 19th Century. In: The Indian Geographer. Vol. 9, Nr. 1 and 2. New Delhi, pp. 67-82.

STEWIG, R. (1965): The Development of Road Communications between Central Europe and the Orient via Beograd, Sofiya, Istanbul. In: Geografia. A Research Journal of Geography. Pakistan Institute of Geography. Vol. IV. Nr. 1 and 2. Karachi, pp. 1-10.

STEWIG, R. (1966): Bemerkungen zur Entstehung des orientalischen Sackgassengrundrisses am Beispiel der Stadt Istanbul. In: Mitteilungen der Österreichischen Geographischen Gesellschaft zu Wien. Vol. 108. Wien, pp. 25-47.

STEWIG, R. (1970): Bursa, Nordwestanatolien. Strukturwandel einer orientalischen Stadt unter dem Einfluß der Industrialisierung. Schriften des Geographischen Instituts der Universität Kiel, Vol. 32. Kiel.

STEWIG, R. (1972): Die Industrialisierung in der Türkei. In: Die Erde. 103. year. Berlin, pp. 21-47.
STEWIG, R. (1986): Bursa, Nordwestanatolien. Auswirkungen der Industrialisierung auf die Bevölkerungs- und Sozialstruktur einer Industriegroßstadt im Orient. Part 2. Kieler Geographische Schriften. Vol. 65. Kiel.
STEWIG, R. (1986): The Conditions of Endogenous Tourism in the Istanbul Area. In: Türkiye Turing ve Otomobil Kurumu Belleteni 74/353. Istanbul, pp. 64-66.
STEWIG, R. (1998): Wandlungen einer byzantinischen Zisterne in der Altstadt von Istanbul. In: Materialia Turcica. Vol 19. Göttingen, pp. 69-76.
STEWIG, R. (1998): Entstehung der Industriegesellschaft in der Türkei. Part 1: Entwicklung bis 1950. Kieler Geographische Schriften. Vol 96. Kiel.
STEWIG, R. (1999): Entstehung der Industriegesellschaft in der Türkei. Part 2: Entwicklung 1950-1980. Kieler Geographische Schriften. Vol. 99. Kiel.
STEWIG, R. (2000): Entstehung der Industriegesellschaft in der Türkei. Part 3: Entwicklung seit 1980. Kieler Geographische Schriften. Vol. 102. Kiel.
STEWIG, R. (2003): Bursa, Nordwestanatolien: 30 Jahre danach. Kieler Geographische Schriften. Vol. 107. Kiel.
STEWIG, R. (2004): Die Türkei auf dem Weg von der Agrar- zur Industriegesellschaft. In: Orient. Vol. 45. Wiesbaden, pp. 125-140.
STEWIG, R. (2004): Proposal for Including Bursa, the Cradle City of the Ottoman Empire, in the UNESCO World Heritage Inventory. Kieler Geographische Schriften. Vol. 108. Kiel.
STEWIG, R. (2006): Traffic Functions of the Bosphorus. In: Orient. Vol. 47. Baden-Baden, pp. 97-118.
STEWIG, R. (2006): Entwicklung der innerstädtischen Verkehrserschließung Istanbuls im Spiegel gesellschaftlicher Transformation in der Türkei. In: GANS, P. & A. PRIEBS, R. WEHRHAHN (eds.): Kulturgeographie der Stadt. Festschrift für J. Bähr. Kieler Geographische Schriften. Vol. 111. Kiel, pp. 605-633.
STEWIG, R. & E. TÜMERTEKIN, B. TOLUN, R. TURFAN, D. WIEBE and students (1980): Bursa, Nordwestanatolien. Auswirkungen der Industrialisierung auf die Bevölkerungs- und Sozialstruktur einer Industriegroßstadt im Orient. Part 1. Kieler Geographische Schriften. Vol. 51. Kiel.
SUMNER-BOYD, M. & J. FREELY (1972): Strolling Through Istanbul. A Guide to the City. Istanbul.
SWEETMAN, B. (2001): The Crimean War. Oxford. (Osprey Series: Essential Histories).
TCHIHATCEFF, P. de (1864): Le Bosphore et Constantinople. Paris.
TEDSTONE, T. E. (1986): Steam on the Bosphorus. In: Ships Monthly 21, 9. Burton-on-Trent, pp. 28-31.
TEMEL MÜHENDISLIK A. S. (1986): The Master Plan for the Bosphorus Area. Interim Report. Istanbul, London.

TUCHELT, K. (1962): Uferpaläste osmanischer Zeit am Bosporus. In: Institut für Auslandsbeziehungen. Zeitschrift für Kulturaustausch. Vol. 12, 2/3. Stuttgart, pp. 168-178.

TÜMERTEKIN, E. (1970-1971): Manufacturing and Suburbanization in Istanbul. In: Review of the Geographical Institute of the University of Istanbul. International Edition. Nr. 13. Istanbul, pp. 1-40.

TÜMERTEKIN, E. (1974-1976): Industry as a Factor of Modification of the Geographical Landscape of the Bosphorus. In: Review of the Geographical Institute of the University of Istanbul.International Edition. Nr. 15. Istanbul, pp. 1-28.

TÜMERTEKIN, E. (2000): Istanbul: une métropole anatolienne. In: BALLAND, D. (ed): Hommes et Terres d'Islam. Mélanges offerts a Xavier de Planhol. Vol. 2. Bibliothèque Iranienne 53. Téhéran, pp. 133-141. (Institut Français de Recherche en Iran).

TUĞLACI, P. (1992): The Role of the Dalyan Family in Ottoman Architecture. Istanbul.

TUROĞLU, H. (1996): Morpho-Tectonic Evolution of the Izmit-Sapanca Trough (Western Anatolia). In: Review of the Department of Geography of the University of Istanbul. International Edition. Nr. 3. Istanbul, pp. 135-150.

UNESCO World Heritage Centre (1972): Convention Concerning the Protection of the World Cultural and Natural Heritage. Paris.

UNESCO World Heritage Centre (1999): Operational Guidelines for the Implementation of the World Heritage Convention. Paris.

UNESCO World Heritage Centre (2005): Operational Guidelines for the Implementation of the World Heritage Convention. Paris.

YERASIMOS, St. (2000): Constantinople. De Byzance à Istanbul. Paris.

YERASIMOS, St. (2000): Konstantinopel. Istanbuls historisches Erbe. Köln.

ZIYA, M. (I. 1920; II. 1928): Istanbul ve Boğaziçi. Bizans ve Osmanlı medeniyetlerinin asarı bakiyısı. Istanbul.

9 Photographic Documentation

All photos taken by the author between 1959 and 2006.

Two aspects are combined in the photographic documention.

It is true, the various objects depicted – monuments, buildings, houses and other features – all have a value of their own which is connected with their function, their structure, their style and architecture. But all these objects do not merely stand for themselves, they are – in this publication – seen as part of the Bosphorus sea- and landscape. So the one aspect which is being followed is their spatial position within the Bosphorus sea- and landscape, their setting.

The other aspect is the historical one. This aspect has been one of the guidelines for the verbal delineation of the cultural features of the Bosphorus sea- and landscape. Its historical character and the author's long acquaintance with the area – since 1959 – allows the inclusion of some historical photos – of the second half of the 20^h century – in the photographic documentation.

Photo 1: The southern entrance to the Bosphorus (left) and the Golden Horn

Photo 2: The first Bosphorus bridge (from 1973)

Photo 3: The second Bosphorus bridge (from 1988) and the crooked bay of Istinye
Source: All three photos were taken in 2006 after take-off from Atatürk airport.

Photo 4: The lower Bosphorus and the entrance to the Golden Horn (left), 1959

Photo 5: The lower Bosphorus and the entrance to the Golden Horn (left), 2006
Both photos were taken from the Beyazıt/Serasker/University tower.

Photographic Documentation 81

Photo 6: The Dolmabahçe palace; in the background international hotels, 2006

Photo 7: The central section of the Dolmabahçe palace, 1959

Photo 8: The Dolmabahçe mosque, 1959

Photo 9: The Dolmabahçe clock tower, 1997

Photographic Documentation 83

Photo 10: The Çırağan palace as a ruin, 1959

Photo 11: The Çırağan palace as a noble hotel, 2000

Photo 12: The Beylerbeyi palace, dwarfed by the first Bosphorus bridge, 2000

Photo 13: The Küçüksu palace, 2006

Photographic Documentation

Photo 14: Section of Rumeli Hisarı, 1962

Photo 15: Rumeli Hisarı, 2006

Photo 16: Anadolu Hisarı behind several yalıs (from right to left): Komodor Remzi Paşa yalı, İlyas Bey / Pink yalı, Şeyh Talat Efendi yalı (being renovated), Manastırlı İsmail Hakkı Bey yalı, Köseleçiler yalı, 2066

Photographic Documentation

Photo 17: Ruin of the Genoese castle (Yoros) above Anadolu Kavağı and the Marko Paşa villa in the Turkish naval base, 2006

Photo 18: Tophane (left), Nusretiye mosque (middle) and Kılıç Ali Paşa mosque (right), cut off from the Bosphorus by the new Salıpazarı quay, 2006. Photo taken from the Galata Kulesi.

Photographic Documentation

Photo 20: Kışlası barracks above the container port at Harem – Haydarpaşa, 2006

Photo 22: The Haydarpaşa railway station, 2006

Photo 19: Kuleli Askeri Lisesi and Kuleli mosque below Büyük Çamlıca, 2006

Photo 21: The building of the Marmara University above the port of Istanbul at Harem – Haydarpaşa, 2006

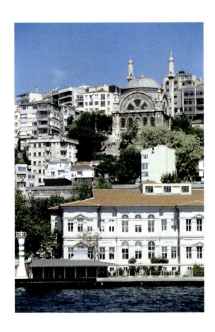

Photo 23: The Cihangir mosque in the Fındıklı Kabataş section, 2006

Photo 24: The Haydarpaşa mosque, 2006

Photographic Documentation 91

Photo 25: The Şemsi Paşa mosque, at the water, and the Rum Mehmet Paşa mosque at Usküdar, 2006

Photo 26: The Iskender Paşa mosque and a radar surveillance tower at the Kanlıca landing stage, 2006

Photo 27: Arnavutköy, 1959

Photo 28: Arnavutköy, 2006

Photo 29: The oldest existing yalı, the Amcazade Hüseyin Paşa Köprülü yalı in a dilapidated state, south of the second Bosphorus bridge, 2006

Photo 30: The Sait Halim Paşa yalı, Yeniköy, 2006

Photo 31: The Şehzade Burhanettin Efendi yalı, Yeniköy, 2006

Photographic Documentation

Photo 32: The Ahmet Afif Paşa yalı, Yeniköy, 2006

Photo 33: The Feridun yalı, Yeniköy, 2006

Photographic Documentation

Photo 34: Modern yalıs at Kandilli, below the Kandilli Kız Lisesi (ex Adile Sultan palace), 2006

Photographic Documentation

Photo 36: The restored palace of Abas Hilmi Paşa, the former Khedive (viceroy) of Egypt, at Kanlica, 1985

Photo 35: The Asaf Paşa yalı (redbrown) and the Ahmet Rasim Paşa yalı (left) below the ex Khedive (viceroy) summer palace at Kanlica, 2006

Photo 37: Yalıs in a row, at the water; Yeniköy, 2006

Photo 38: Summer residence of the Austrian ambassy, south of Tarabya, 2006

Photo 39: Summer residence of the German ambassy, south of Tarabya, 2006

Photo 40: Summer residence of the Russian ambassy, Sariyer, 2006

Photographic Documentation

Photo 42: Tourists at the landing stage of Sarıyer, 2006

Photo 44: Waterside promenade between Üsküdar and Harem; Kız Kulesi and Topkapı Sarayı 2006

Photo 41: Recreation at the landing stage of Kanlıca, 2006

Photo 43: Recreation at the landing stage of Ortaköy, 2006

Photo 46: Pilot and fire fighting vessels at the bay of Istinye, 2006

Photo 48: Tankfarm at Çubuklu, 1985

Photo 45: Dalyan (stationary installation) for catching fish, bay of Beykoz, 1959

Photo 47: Paşabahçe glass factory, 2006

Ältere Bände der
Schriften des Geographischen Instituts der Universität Kiel
(Band I, 1932 - Band 43, 1975)
sowie der
Kieler Geographischen Schriften
(Band 44, 1976 - Band 57, 1983)
sind teilweise noch auf Anfrage im Geographischen Institut der CAU erhältlich

Band 58
Bähr, Jürgen (Hrsg.): Kiel 1879 - 1979. Entwicklung von Stadt und Umland im Bild der Topographischen Karte 1:25 000. Zum 32. Deutschen Kartographentag vom 11. - 14. Mai 1983 in Kiel. 1983. III, 192 S., 21 Tab., 38 Abb. mit 2 Kartenblättern in Anlage. ISBN 3-923887-00-0. 14,30 €

Band 59
Gans, Paul: Raumzeitliche Eigenschaften und Verflechtungen innerstädtischer Wanderungen in Ludwigshafen/Rhein zwischen 1971 und 1978. Eine empirische Analyse mit Hilfe des Entropiekonzeptes und der Informationsstatistik. 1983. XII, 226 S., 45 Tab. und 41 Abb. ISBN 3-923887-01-9. 15,30 €

Band 60
*Paffen, Karlheinz und Kortum, Gerhard: Die Geographie des Meeres. Disziplingeschichtliche Entwicklung seit 1650 und heutiger methodischer Stand. 1984. XIV, 293 S., 25 Abb. ISBN 3-923887-02-7.

Band 61
*Bartels, Dietrich u. a.: Lebensraum Norddeutschland. 1984. IX, 139 S., 23 Tab. und 21 Karten. ISBN 3-923887-03-5.

Band 62
Klug, Heinz (Hrsg.): Küste und Meeresboden. Neue Ergebnisse geomorphologischer Feldforschungen. 1985. V, 214 S., 45 Fotos, 10 Tab.und 66 Abb.
ISBN 3-923887-04-3. 19,90 €

Band 63
Kortum, Gerhard: Zuckerrübenanbau und Entwicklung ländlicher Wirtschaftsräume in der Türkei. Ausbreitung und Auswirkung einer Industriepflanze unter besonderer Berücksichtigung des Bezirks Beypazari (Provinz Ankara). 1986. XVI, 392 S., 36 Tab., 47 Abb. und 8 Fotos im Anhang. ISBN 3-923887-05-1. 23,00 €

Band 64
Fränzle, Otto (Hrsg.): Geoökologische Umweltbewertung. Wissenschaftstheoretische und methodische Beiträge zur Analyse und Planung. 1986. VI,130 S., 26 Tab. und 30 Abb. ISBN 3-923887-06-X. 12,30 €

Band 65
Stewig, Reinhard: Bursa, Nordwestanatolien. Auswirkungen der Industrialisierung auf die Bevölkerungs- und Sozialstruktur einer Industriegroßstadt im Orient. Teil 2. 1986. XVI, 222 S., 71 Tab., 7 Abb. und 20 Fotos. ISBN 3-923887-07-8
19,00 €

Band 66
Stewig, Reinhard (Hrsg.): Untersuchungen über die Kleinstadt in Schleswig-Holstein. 1987. VI, 370 S., 38 Tab., 11 Diagr. und 84 Karten
ISBN 3-923887-08-6. 24,50 €

Band 67
Achenbach, Hermann: Historische Wirtschaftskarte des östlichen Schleswig-Holstein um 1850. XII, 277 S., 38 Tab., 34 Abb., Textband und Kartenmappe.
ISBN 3-923887-09-4. 34,30 €

*= vergriffen

Band 68
Bähr, Jürgen (Hrsg.): Wohnen in lateinamerikanischen Städten - Housing in Latin American cities. 1988. IX, 299 S., 64 Tab., 71 Abb. und 21 Fotos.
ISBN 3-923887-10-8. 22,50 €

Band 69
Baudissin-Zinzendorf, Ute Gräfin von: Freizeitverkehr an der Lübecker Bucht. Eine gruppen- und regionsspezifische Analyse der Nachfrageseite. 1988. XII, 350 S., 50 Tab., 40 Abb. und 4 Abb. im Anhang. ISBN 3-923887-11-6. 16,40 €

Band 70
Härtling, Andrea: Regionalpolitische Maßnahmen in Schweden. Analyse und Bewertung ihrer Auswirkungen auf die strukturschwachen peripheren Landesteile. 1988. IV, 341 Seiten, 50 Tab., 8 Abb. und 16 Karten. ISBN 3-923887-12-4.
15,70 €

Band 71
Pez, Peter: Sonderkulturen im Umland von Hamburg. Eine standortanalytische Untersuchung. 1989. XII, 190 S., 27 Tab. und 35 Abb. ISBN 3-923887-13-2.
11,40 €

Band 72
Kruse, Elfriede: Die Holzveredelungsindustrie in Finnland. Struktur- und Standortmerkmale von 1850 bis zur Gegenwart. 1989. X, 123 S., 30 Tab., 26 Abb. und 9 Karten.
ISBN 3-923887-14-0. 12,60 €

Band 73
Bähr, Jürgen, Christoph Corves und Wolfram Noodt (Hrsg.): Die Bedrohung tropischer Wälder: Ursachen, Auswirkungen, Schutzkonzepte. 1989. IV, 149 S., 9 Tab. und 27 Abb. ISBN 3-923887-15-9 13,20 €

Band 74
Bruhn, Norbert: Substratgenese - Rumpfflächendynamik. Bodenbildung und Tiefenverwitterung in saprolitisch zersetzten granitischen Gneisen aus Südindien. 1990. IV, 191 S. 35 Tab., 31 Abb. und 28 Fotos.
ISBN 3-923887-16-7. 11,60 €

Band 75
Priebs, Axel: Dorfbezogene Politik und Planung in Dänemark unter sich wandelnden gesellschaftlichen Rahmenbedingungen. 1990. IX, 239 S., 5 Tab. und 28 Abb.
ISBN 3-923887-17-5. 17,30 €

Band 76
Stewig, Reinhard: Über das Verhältnis der Geographie zur Wirklichkeit und zu den Nachbarwissenschaften. Eine Einführung. 1990. IX, 131 S., 15 Abb.
IBSN 923887-18-3. 12,80 €

Band 77
Gans, Paul: Die Innenstädte von Buenos Aires und Montevideo. Dynamik der Nutzungsstruktur, Wohnbedingungen und informeller Sektor. 1990. XVIII, 252 S., & 64 Tab., 36 Abb. und 30 Karten in separatem Kartenband. ISBN 3-923887-19-1.
45,00 €

Band 78
Bähr, Jürgen & Paul Gans (eds): The Geographical Approach to Fertility. 1991. XII, 452 S., 84 Tab. und 167 Fig. ISBN 3-923887-20-5.
22,40 €

Band 79
Reiche, Ernst-Walter: Entwicklung, Validierung und Anwendung eines Modellsystems zur Beschreibung und flächenhaften Bilanzierung der Wasser- und Stickstoffdynamik in Böden. 1991. XIII, 150 S., 27 Tab. und 57 Abb.
ISBN 3-923887-21-3. 9,70 €

Band 80
Achenbach, Hermann (Hrsg.): Beiträge zur regionalen Geographie von Schleswig-Holstein. Festschrift Reinhard Stewig. 1991. X, 386 S., 54 Tab. und 73 Abb.
ISBN 3-923887-22-1. 19,10 €

Band 81
Stewig, Reinhard (Hrsg.): Endogener Tourismus. 1991. V, 193 S., 53 Tab. und 44 Abb.
ISBN 3-923887-23-X. 16,80 €

Band 82
Jürgens, Ulrich: Gemischtrassige Wohngebiete in südafrikanischen Städten. 1991. XVII, 299 S., 58 Tab. und 28 Abb. ISBN 3-923887-24-8. 13,80 €

Band 83
Eckert, Markus: Industrialisierung und Entindustrialisierung in Schleswig-Holstein. 1992. XVII, 350 S., 31 Tab. und 42 Abb
ISBN 3-923887-25-6. 12,70 €

Band 84
Neumeyer, Michael: Heimat. Zu Geschichte und Begriff eines Phänomens. 1992. V, 150 S. ISBN 3-923887-26-4. 9.00 €

Band 85
Kuhnt, Gerald und Zölitz-Möller, Reinhard (Hrsg): Beiträge zur Geoökologie aus Forschung, Praxis und Lehre. Otto Fränzle zum 60. Geburtstag. 1992. VIII, 376 S., 34 Tab. und 88 Abb. ISBN 3-923887-27-2. 19,00 €

Band 86
Reimers, Thomas: Bewirtschaftungsintensität und Extensivierung in der Landwirtschaft. Eine Untersuchung zum raum-, agrar- und betriebsstrukturellen Umfeld am Beispiel Schleswig-Holsteins. 1993. XII, 232 S., 44 Tab., 46 Abb. und 12 Klappkarten im Anhang.
ISBN 3-923887-28-0. 12,20 €

Band 87
Stewig, Reinhard (Hrsg.): Stadtteiluntersuchungen in Kiel, Baugeschichte, Sozialstruktur, Lebensqualität, Heimatgefühl. 1993. VIII, 337 S., 159 Tab., 10 Abb., 33 Karten und 77 Graphiken. ISBN 923887-29-9. 12.30 €

Band 88
Wichmann, Peter: Jungquartäre randtropische Verwitterung. Ein bodengeographischer Beitrag zur Landschaftsentwicklung von Südwest-Nepal. 1993. X, 125 S., 18Tab. und 17 Abb. ISBN 3-923887-30-2. 10.10 €

Band 89
Wehrhahn, Rainer: Konflikte zwischen Naturschutz und Entwicklung im Bereich des Atlantischen Regenwaldes im Bundesstaat São Paulo, Brasilien. Untersuchungen zur Wahrnehmung von Umweltproblemen und zur Umsetzung von Schutzkonzepten. 1994. XIV, 293 S., 72 Tab., 41 Abb. und 20 Fotos. ISBN 3-923887-31-0. 17,50 €

Band 90
Stewig, Reinhard (Hrsg.): Entstehung und Entwicklung der Industriegesellschaft auf den Britischen Inseln. 1995. XII, 367 S., 20 Tab., 54 Abb. und 5 Graphiken.
ISBN 3-923887-32-9. 16,60 €

Band 91
Bock, Steffen: Ein Ansatz zur polygonbasierten Klassifikation von Luft- und Satellitenbildern mittels künstlicher neuronaler Netze. 1995. XI, 152 S., 4 Tab. und 48 Abb.
ISBN 3-923887-33-7. 8,60 €

Band 92
Matuschewski, Anke: Stadtentwicklung durch Public-Private-Partnership in Schweden. Kooperationsansätze der achtziger und neunziger Jahre im Vergleich. 1996. XI, 246 S., 16 Tab., 34 Abb., und 20 Fotos.
ISBN 3-923887-34-5. 12,20 €

Band 93
Ulrich, Johannes und Kortum, Gerhard.: Otto Krümmel (1854-1912): Geograph und Wegbereiter der modernen Ozeanographie. 1997. VIII, 340 S. ISBN 3-923887-35-3.
24,00 €

Band 94
Schenck, Freya S.: Strukturveränderungen spanisch-amerikanischer Mittelstädte untersucht am Beispiel der Stadt Cuenca, Ecuador. 1997. XVIII, 270 S.
ISBN 3-923887-36-1.
13,20 €

Band 95
Pez, Peter: Verkehrsmittelwahl im Stadtbereich und ihre Beeinflussbarkeit. Eine verkehrsgeographische Analyse am Beispiel Kiel und Lüneburg. 1998. XVII, 396 S., 52 Tab. und 86 Abb.
ISBN 3-923887-37-X.
17,30 €

Band 96
Stewig, Reinhard: Entstehung der Industriegesellschaft in der Türkei. Teil 1: Entwicklung bis 1950, 1998. XV, 349 S., 35 Abb., 4 Graph., 5 Tab. und 4 Listen.
ISBN 3-923887-38-8.
15,40 €

Band 97
Higelke, Bodo (Hrsg.): Beiträge zur Küsten- und Meeresgeographie. Heinz Klug zum 65. Geburtstag gewidmet von Schülern, Freunden und Kollegen. 1998. XXII, 338 S., 29 Tab., 3 Fotos und 2 Klappkarten. ISBN 3-923887-39-6.
18,40 €

Band 98
Jürgens, Ulrich: Einzelhandel in den Neuen Bundesländern - die Konkurrenzsituation zwischen Innenstadt und "Grüner Wiese", dargestellt anhand der Entwicklungen in Leipzig, Rostock und Cottbus. 1998. XVI. 395 S., 83 Tab. und 52 Abb.
ISBN 3-923887-40-X.
16,30 €

Band 99
Stewig, Reinhard: Entstehung der Industriegesellschaft in der Türkei. Teil 2: Entwicklung 1950-1980. 1999. XI, 289 S., 36 Abb., 8 Graph., 12 Tab. und 2 Listen.
ISBN 3-923887-41-8.
13,80 €

Band 100
Eglitis, Andri: Grundversorgung mit Gütern und Dienstleistungen in ländlichen Räumen der neuen Bundesländer. Persistenz und Wandel der dezentralen Versorgungsstrukturen seit der deutschen Einheit. 1999. XXI, 422 S., 90 Tab. und 35 Abb.
ISBN 3-923887-42-6.
20,60 €

Band 101
Dünckmann, Florian: Naturschutz und kleinbäuerliche Landnutzung im Rahmen Nachhaltiger Entwicklung. Untersuchungen zu regionalen und lokalen Auswirkungen von umweltpolitischen Maßnahmen im Vale do Ribeira, Brasilien. 1999. XII, 294 S., 10 Tab., 9 Karten und 1 Klappkarte.ISBN 3-923887-43-4.
23,40 €

Band 102
Stewig, Reinhard: Entstehung der Industriegesellschaft in der Türkei. Teil 3: Entwicklung seit 1980. 2000. XX, 360 S., 65 Tab., 12 Abb. und 5 Graphiken
ISBN 3-923887-44-2.
17,10 €

Band 103
Bähr, Jürgen & Widderich, Sönke: Vom Notstand zum Normalzustand - eine Bilanz des kubanischen Transformationsprozesses. La larga marcha desde el período especial habia la normalidad - un balance de la transformación cubana. 2000. XI, 222 S., 51 Tab. und 15 Abb. ISBN 3-923887-45-0.
11,40 €

Band 104
Bähr, Jürgen & Jürgens, Ulrich: Transformationsprozesse im Südlichen Afrika - Konsequenzen für Gesellschaft und Natur. Symposium in Kiel vom 29.10.-30.10.1999. 2000. 222 S., 40 Tab., 42 Abb. und 2 Fig.
ISBN 3-923887-46-9.
13,30 €

Band 105
Gnad, Martin: Desegregation und neue Segregation in Johannesburg nach dem Ende der Apartheid. 2002. 281 S., 28 Tab. und 55 Abb.
ISBN 3-923887-47-7. 14,80 €

Band 106
*Widderich, Sönke: Die sozialen Auswirkungen des kubanischen Transformationsprozesses. 2002. 210 S., 44 Tab. und 17 Abb. ISBN 3-923887-48-5. 12,55 €

Band 107
Stewig, Reinhard: Bursa, Nordwestanatolien: 30 Jahre danach. 2003. 163 S., 16 Tab., 20 Abb. und 20 Fotos.ISBN 3-923887-49-3. 13,00 €

Band 108
Stewig, Reinhard: Proposal for Including Bursa, the Cradle City of the Ottoman Empire, in the UNESCO Wolrd Heritage Inventory. 2004. X, 75 S., 21 Abb., 16 Farbfotos und 3 Pläne. ISBN 3-923887-50-7. 18,00 €

Band 109
Rathje, Frank: Umnutzungsvorgänge in der Gutslandschaft von Schleswig-Holstein und Mecklenburg-Vorpommern. Eine Bilanz unter der besonderen Berücksichtigung des Tourismus. 2004. VI, 330 S., 56 Abb. ISBN 3-923887-51-5. 18,20 €

Band 110
Matuschewski, Anke: Regionale Verankerung der Informationswirtschaft in Deutschland. Materielle und immaterielle Beziehungen von Unternehmen der Informationswirtschaft in Dresden-Ostsachsen, Hamburg und der TechnologieRegion Karlsruhe. 2004. II, 385 S., 71 Tab. und 30 Abb. ISBN 3-923887-52-3. 18,00 €

Band 111
Gans, Paul, Axel Priebs und Rainer Wehrhahn (Hrsg.): Kulturgeographie der Stadt. 2006. VI, 646 S., 65 Tab. und 110 Abb.
ISBN 3-923887-53-1. 34,00 €

Band 112
Plöger, Jörg: Die nachträglich abgeschotteten Nachbarschaften in Lima (Peru). Eine Analyse sozialräumlicher Kontrollmaßnahmen im Kontext zunehmender Unsicherheiten. 2006. VI, 202 S., 1 Tab. und 22 Abb. ISBN 3-923887-54-X. 14,50 €

Band 113
Stewig, Reinhard: Proposal for Including the Bosphorus, a Singularly Integrated Natural, Cultural and Historical Sea- and Landscape, in the UNESCO World Heritage Inventory. 2007. VII, 102 S., 5 Abb. und 48 Farbfotos. ISBN 3-923887-55-8. 19,50 €